The Writings of
Paul Frees

The Writings of
Paul Frees
Scripts and Songs from the Master of Voice

Edited by Ben Ohmart

BearManor Media
2004

The Writings of Paul Frees:
Scripts and Songs From the Master of Voice

All scripts & lyrics © The Paul Frees Estate
Editor's Note © Ben Ohmart
All rights reserved.

Published in the USA by
Bear Manor Media
P.O. Box 750
Boalsburg PA 16827

bearmanormedia.com

Cover design by John Teehan
Typesetting and layout by John Teehan

ISBN 1-59393-011-9

Table of Contents

A Word From the Editor i

The Demon From Dimension X 1
  screenplay

Lyrics 145

Partners In Crime 159
  a television treatment

Who Knows 161
  an audition script for television

A Word from the Editor

One of the most surprising byproducts of constructing my biography, *Welcome, Foolish Mortals... The Life and Voices of Paul Frees*, was coming across a voluminous stash of Frees-written material: a box of treasures that was almost tossed out after Paul's death. Within this package, which I was most graciously loaned, were photos and scripts, most of which have never been seen before, even by the Frees family. The photos were amazing, but the scripts were completely unexpected. Everyone knows what a prolific voice man Paul Frees was, but few people know Paul the *very* prolific writer.

Assembled here is a mere portion of his lucrative output. If it had been possible to track down the families of his various collaborators and secure permission to include some of his other goodies, this book would be twice this size or in several volumes. But what is here is to be savored, giving us another glimpse of a very singular, unstoppable talent.

Thanks to Jordan R. Young for providing the material written for Spike Jones, and loud applause to the Frees family, Peter Davis, Joyce Post, Laura Wagner, and my always supportive parents.

Ben Ohmart
August 2004

THE DEMON FROM DIMENSION X

FADE-IN:

1.   INT. OPERATING ROOM – CLOSE-UP – NIGHT

MUSIC sets an ominous low-key mood as we fade-in on a long rack of test tubes, beakers and connected glass paraphernalia. Chemicals are flowing through this maze of bubbling, foaming laboratory equipment. We hear the BLOOP, BLEEPING SOUND of the liquid as it courses through the "Rube Goldberg"-type setup...Now the CAMERA PULLS BACK to reveal a bearded scientist in a white smock. He is busy pouring bubbling liquid from one vial to another...He fills a large hypodermic needle with it and we PULL BACK even further to reveal a beautiful young nurse standing next to an operating table. The nurse is intently watching a cloth the size of a small towel in the center of the table...The cloth is draped over "something" that moves and jerks spasmodically! Now the bearded SCIENTIST walks over to the table holding the needle in readiness...The MUSIC builds as he nods to the NURSE to remove the cloth. With a grandiose sweep she *pulls* the cover from the table to reveal the gnarled...scaly, SEVERED arm and hand of some terrifying MONSTER!...Now the CAMERA ZOOMS in for a full CLOSE-UP of the arm that *fills* the screen!...The MUSIC hits a terrifying crescendo. The arm twitches and scratches feebly as we HOLD ON IT to SUPERIMPOSE TITLES!...

THE DEMON FROM DIMENSION X

We HOLD ON ARM through END SUPER TITLES, and PULL BACK TO:

2.   MED. SHOT

The Scientist looks at the Nurse.

> NURSE
> We better hurry, sir, it's getting weaker!

The doctor nods, moves in and shoots needle into arm.

> SCIENTIST
> There...it's done...
> *(wipes brow)*
> We'll know in a moment!

MUSIC PLAYS A VARIATION OF "$64,000 QUESTION" -type suspense theme...we MOVE IN TO TIGHT SHOT of Nurse and arm...The arm is perfectly still; it doesn't move!

> NURSE
> *(Eyes widening)*
> Doctor! It's moving—It's getting *stronger*!
> Look at it MOVE!

As she says this, we ARE HOLDING THE ARM IN CLOSE-UP, and notice that it doesn't move at all! It just lays there!

> NURSE
> It's reaching out to *get* me!

BUT THE ARM HASN'T MOVED AT ALL! Now the Nurse falters in her speech.

> NURSE
> It's *moving*...It's mov...

Now she looks up directly INTO THE CAMERA. She has a confused expression on her face.

> NURSE
> It's *moving!*

Now the CAMERA PULLS BACK to a LONG SHOT to reveal that the laboratory is a MOTION PICTURE set! We see the lights, the grips, the camera crew, sound, etc., as the Director walks onto the set...

> DIRECTOR
> Cut!...CUT!...Nice try, Helen
> *(He laughs)*
> All right, somebody help Charlie!

3. MED. SHOT—SET AND TABLE

An assistant goes to the table, lifts the arm, and pushes it through a hole in the tabletop as the DIRECTOR lifts the curtain that surrounds the base of the operating table.

4. TWO-SHOT—DIRECTOR AND CHARLIE

As the Director parts the curtain, a little guy comes out from under the table. On one arm, he has a "horrible" severed arm—it's rubber!

> DIRECTOR
> Charlie! You were supposed to move the arm
> and reach for Helen! What happened?

> CHARLIE
> I'm sorry, my arm fell asleep!

> DIRECTOR
> *(Slaps him on the back)*
> S'alright, Charlie.
> *(Calls)*
> Bill! The take before this one was okay, wasn't it?

> ASST. DIRECTOR, BILL
> *(Walks into the scene)*
> Yeah.

> DIRECTOR
> Let's use it, it's getting too late for another shot. Give 'em their calls for Monday.

> ASST. DIRECTOR
> Right.
> *(Loudly)*
> Brownstone Street Monday.

Director walks over to Helen.

> DIRECTOR
> I guess that finishes you, Helen. Nice job, for what it was.

> HELEN
> *(Taking off hat)*
> Thanks, Jerry.

> DIRECTOR
> I got another one of these turkeys coming up soon. I'll give ya a call, okay?

> HELEN
> *(Grateful)*
> Any time.

CAMERA PANS as Helen walks to the side of the set where there's a row of green portable dressing rooms, a makeup table, and a prematurely grey, handsome man standing and smiling as Helen approaches him. He is her fiance, BRAD CURTIS. She kisses him warmly.

> HELEN
> That's for waiting so patiently for me! Were you bored?

> BRAD
> I enjoyed it. You know, I thought making movies

was easy, but it's a lot of work, isn't it?

                HELEN
These things are fun.

They are interrupted by little Charlie who comes over to Helen.

               CHARLIE
Gee, I'm sorry I loused up that last shot, Helen, my arm…fell…

                HELEN
          (Understandingly)
I know, you couldn't help it, Charlie…wasn't your fault.

               CHARLIE
Y'know, holding my arm like that it just fell…

                BRAD
It isn't easy to do that.
        (Helen turns to Brad)

                HELEN
Oh, I'm sorry. This is my fiancé, Doctor Curtis. Honey, this is Charlie, uh, I never did know your last name, Charlie.

               CHARLIE
            (Smiling)
Jus' Charlie, thas good enuf. A doctor, huh? Lookie here, Doc…
            (Lifts arm)
Think I hurt somethin'—it's all red.

                BRAD
I'm afraid I can't help you. I'm not a medical doctor.

HELEN
Brad's a Doctor of Physics, Charlie,
at the University!

CHARLIE
Ooooh! No kiddin'—a scientist like, huh?

BRAD
(Modestly)
Kind of...
(Looks at his watch)
Look honey, if we're gonna make it up the hill
before dark, we better hurry.

HELEN
Oh, golly, I almost forgot.

She starts for the first dressing room next to the makeup table where they're standing.

HELEN
(Continues)
I'll change right away. Charlie, mind keeping
Brad company for a minute?

CHARLIE
Glad to, I gotta wait for makeup to help me get
outta this arm!

CUT TO:

5. INT. FRONT OF THE DRESSING ROOM—CLOSE-UP

Helen goes in, sticks her head around the door, and smiles at Brad.

HELEN
Just be a minute, honey!

Puckers mouth and blows him a kiss.

CUT TO:

6.   BRAD AND CHARLIE—TWO-SHOT

>   CHARLIE
> She's a nice kid!

>   BRAD
>   *(Warmly)*
> I think so!

>   CHARLIE
>   *(Holds up arm, scratches at it)*
> Sure wish Morris would get here an' get this thing offa me. It's startin' to itch somethin' terrible.

>   BRAD
>   *(Attentively)*
> I imagine so.

>   HELEN *(O.C.)*
> Brad!

Brad looks toward the dressing room.

>   BRAD
> Yeah?

CUT TO:

7.   CLOSE-UP—HELEN AT DOOR

Her head is poked around the door.

>   HELEN
> What should I wear?

CUT TO:

8.   BRAD CLOSE-UP

                      BRAD
I don't know, anything comfortable. It's a two-hour ride to Crystal Springs.

                      HELEN *(O.C.)*
All right.

                      CHARLIE
                     (Inquisitive)
Goin' to Crystal Springs, huh?
                     (Brad nods)
It's nice up there this time of year.

                      BRAD
Yes, it is.

                      CHARLIE
Papers said we got a storm comin'. Hope it don't mess up your vacation.

                      BRAD
                     (Politely)
We're not going for a vacation—I have to work.

                      CHARLIE
Work, no kiddin', what'ya teach, skiing, as a hobby, I mean.

Brad doesn't want to talk, but what's he gonna do…

                      BRAD
No, we, the University that is, has an experimental station up there—a laboratory.

                        CHARLIE
                    (Points to set)
                Not like this one, I hope.

                         BRAD
                    (Laughs lightly)
                Hardly. It's an electronic lab, you know, radio
                frequencies, and uh, tubes and condensers,
                oscilloscopes, you know.

                        CHARLIE
                    (He doesn't know)
                Yeah, I know.

Brad being polite, but looking for help, calls to Helen.

                         BRAD
                You about ready, Helen?

                     HELEN *(O.C.)*
                Just about. Gotta pack a couple of things.

                         BRAD
                (Trying to get away from Charlie)
                Can I help?

                     HELEN (O.C.)
                No, I can manage. You take it easy and talk
                to Charlie.

                         BRAD
                        (Stuck)
                All right.

Looks at Charlie grinning at him.

                        CHARLIE
                She's a nice kid.

                    BRAD
Yeah, nice kid.

                    CHARLIE
So, you two are gettin' hitched, huh?

                    BRAD
Yes, any day now.

                    CHARLIE
You're a lucky guy.

                    BRAD
        (Really getting impatient, but still polite)
Yeah.

Charlie making conversation.

                    CHARLIE
You ain't sneakin' away to the Springs to get hitched, secret like, are ya?
        (Winks)

                    BRAD
No, just to work.

                    CHARLIE
What's she going for then?
                    BRAD
Well, she's never been up there before and she's going to meet my partner, Mike. He's going to be the Best Man at the wedding.

                    CHARLIE
Oh, why don't he come down here?

Brad is at the breaking point; he signs deeply.

                        BRAD
            Because he...

Thank God, Helen comes out. She's got some dresses slung over her shoulder and carries a makeup case.

                        HELEN
            There! See! I'm all ready.

                        BRAD
            That's great. We gotta hurry. Charlie here
            says it might rain.

                        HELEN
            Well, let's go—here grab these!

He takes the wardrobe from her.

                        CHARLIE
            Well, sure nice meetin' up with ya, Doc.

                        BRAD
                    (Relieved they're going)
            It was nice meetin' up with you, Charlie.

Charlie sticks out his hand to shake—it's the monster hand.

                        CHARLIE
                        (Joking)
            Pardon the glove!

                        HELEN
            Bye, Charlie—see you soon!

                        CHARLIE
            Yeah.
                        (Confidential)
            You won't forget to talk to Jerry for me like ya said.

                        HELEN
            Don't worry, I won't.

They walk away and toward the door.

                        BRAD
            What was that about?

                        HELEN
            Oh, I promised him I'd talk to the Director about
            a part in the next picture—a talking part.

                        BRAD
            A talking part, huh? Well, he can handle it.
            He sure can talk!

They walk out the door as we...

FADE-OUT

FADE-IN

9.   EXT. EXPERIMENTAL LAB AT CRYSTAL SPRINGS – NIGHT

We see a late model Sedan come up the road and pull off to the side of the cabin that houses the Experimental Lab. It's a thickly wooded area, surrounding the cabin and just the one dirt road leads up to this isolated place. The cabin itself is a rough lodge-like affair, and only the two 60-foot radio antennas seen to either side of it distinguish it from any other mountain retreat. The car doors open, and we...

CUT TO:

10.   TWO-SHOT – BRAD AND HELEN – EXT. CAR

They get out of the car. Helen stands as Brad reaches in and hands Helen some packages. He picks up a small box of groceries.

BRAD
May as well leave your bags in the car.
I'll drive you down to the Inn soon as we
get straightened out here, okay?

HELEN
You're the boss. Where is the Inn? I thought
you said it was near here.

BRAD
It is.
> *(Points)*

Right through those trees there, see, on that
mountain—see it?

HELEN
> *(Looks)*

No, but I'll take your word for it.
> *(Looks around)*

Gosh, it's quiet up here!

BRAD
Sure it is! That's why we got the Lab here—
no interference, no television, no nothing.

They walk toward the cabin.

HELEN
Where's Mike? He must've heard us drive up!

BRAD
If I know Mike, he didn't hear us 'cause he's
got his head buried in earphones talking
shortwave to China or Alaska—or some place.

HELEN
Brad, do you think he'll like me? I want him to
very much!

>   BRAD
>   *(Confidently)*
>   Don't worry, he will.

11.   WALK THEM TO THE DOOR

They get to the door. Their arms are full of packages. Brad tries the handle—it's locked.

>   BRAD
>   This is a kind of secret project, honey.
>   So remember, you haven't been in here.
>   HELEN
>   *(Cute)*
>   Yes sir.

Brad juggling the packages—bangs on the door with his foot.

>   BRAD
>   Hey! Open up in there. Mike!
>   *(Kicks some more)*
>   Hey Mike!

>   MIKE
>   *(Behind door)*
>   All right! All right, I hear you!

>   HELEN
>   *(Starts to get nervous)*
>   Brad, you sure I look all right? Maybe I
>   should've changed into a dress.

>   BRAD
>   Hey, who are you marrying anyway?
>   You're more worried about him than you are
>   about me!

                            HELEN
                    No, I'm not. It's just…

She is interrupted by the door being unlocked.

12.   EXT. CABIN DOOR – CLOSE-UP

As the door swings open, we see *MIKE*. He is in his late thirties, intelligent, and tall, although it's hard to determine the latter because Mike is confined to a wheelchair. He is an invalid. Mike's face lights up as he sees Helen.

CUT TO:

13.   CLOSE-UP HELEN – MIKE'S POV
Her face registers surprise to see him in a wheelchair and for a moment, she's flustered but she quickly recovers and goes over to him and kisses him on the cheek.

                            HELEN
                          (Warmly)
                        Hi, Mike.

14.   MED. SHOT

                            MIKE
                    Your pictures don't do you justice, Helen.
                    You're beautiful.

                            HELEN
                        Flatterer!

Mike looks over to Brad who stands watching this tableau.

                            MIKE
                    Hey, who's that?

                         HELEN
            Him? Oh, some guy I picked up along the road.

They are all inside now, and Brad kicks the door shut.

15.   INT. CABIN – MED. SHOT – NEW ANGLE

                          BRAD
              If I'm in the way, I'll leave!

Brad walks to the table and dumps the packages on it. Now we see the interior of the cabin. It's a large single room, comfortably decorated in lodge furnishings. A large native stone fireplace takes up the far wall, while one entire corner of the room is devoted to radio transmitters, "ham" equipment, oscilloscopes, and special electronic equipment of all kinds. It's a warm and comfortable room in a state of casual disarray, but in contrast, the "workshop" end of it is neat and orderly.

CUT TO:

16.   TWO-SHOT – HELEN AND MIKE

As he wheels toward the center of the room, she walks along beside him.

                         HELEN
                Where do these groceries go?

                          MIKE
              Just dump 'em on the table. I'll put 'em
              away later.

Helen puts the bundles down and surveys the room.

                         HELEN
                 It's just as I pictured it!

                    MIKE
You mean messy?

                    HELEN
          (Laughs)
Well, it could use a woman's touch here
and there.

Brad has gone over to the side to fill the pipe.

17.   CLOSE-UP—BRAD

                    BRAD
You had better not touch it. If you cleaned
this room up, we'd never find anything!

                    HELEN
You're just two old confirmed bachelors.
I almost hate to break up the set.

                    MIKE
          (Honestly)
You won't be breaking up anything, Helen.
You're just joining the club!

                    HELEN
          (Means it)
You're sweet, Mike—thank you.

Mike at the table picks up some of the packages, goes over to a kitchen arrangement, and starts putting things away, as Brad ambles over to the radio equipment and looks at a few articles on the bench, as he leafs through a logbook.

                    BRAD
How do the new tubes look?

                    MIKE
              (Storing groceries)
        I don't know. I haven't unpacked them yet.
        They're under the bench.

Brad reaches down and brings out two fairly large boxes.

                    BRAD
        Fine, I let you out of my sight for a few hours
        and you goof off! What have you been doing?

                    MIKE
        I've been busy.

                    BRAD
        Doing what? Fiddling with your ham rig, talking
        to Alaska, I'll bet.

                    MIKE
              (Wheels over to Brad)
        Nope, wrong again. I brought in Turkey—and
        guess what, Brad? The guy I was talking to is
        the son of a Prince.

                    BRAD
        So that's what you did all day!

                    MIKE
        Well, we got to talking about the Sputnik and
        our new satellite and which was better—you know.

                    BRAD
        So you never got around to work.

                    MIKE
        Nope, but it was fun. What's the rush anyway?

BRAD
No rush. After all, we've only been waiting six months for the tubes to be built…so…

HELEN
(Interrupts)
Then another night won't make any difference.
(Has on apron)
Now, gentlemen, what will it be for dinner, ham and eggs, steak, tuna…

MIKE
Hold it! Hold it! You're not making dinner.

HELEN
Well, I figured while you boys worked or whatever you're working on, I'd do what a good little wife should do.

MIKE
Well, you're not a lil ol' wife yet and us boys aren't going to work tonight. I'm going to work alone.

BRAD
What are you talking about?

MIKE
What I said, I'm going to work—alone and you two are going over to the Inn and have dinner there alone. Besides, she has to check in at the hotel, doesn't she?

HELEN
I don't mind waiting, honest!

MIKE
Well, I mind. Now you two bundle over, have a

nice quiet dinner, and do a little dancing. It's Friday night, you know.
  (To Helen)
The weekends are big up here!

HELEN
Oh?

BRAD
How we gonna get in without a reservation?

MIKE
I took care of that!

BRAD
I'll bet you did. What else did you take care of?

MIKE
Never mind, just go, man, go!

HELEN
(Looks at Brad)
He's pretty determined to get rid of us, isn't he?

BRAD
Well, if that's the way it's gotta be, I won't fight it. I'm hungry.

SOUND OF ORCHESTRA playing from a distance.

MIKE
Go on now, the music's started already.

BRAD
All right. Look, professor, check those tubes against the diagrams, so maybe tomorrow we can try for "X," ya hear?

MIKE
(Indicates book)
Don't worry, I'll log every frequency and reaction.

BRAD
Reaction? You're not going to use the tubes tonight. Just check 'em!

MIKE
I'll be careful, doctor, don't worry.

BRAD
Please Mike, I'm serious. You can put in the capacitor tubes…
(Brings up box)
…but don't put the juice to them—you promise?

MIKE
You see that Helen? He gives a child a new toy and tells him not to play with it.

HELEN
Well, is it really dangerous?

MIKE
Nah.

BRAD
Yes! That is, I don't know. It could be. It's in a frequency that's never been reached before. Who knows what could happen.

HELEN
Well, Mike, maybe you shouldn't!

MIKE
(Laughing)
What you two doing, ganging up on me?

> Besides, would you deny me the privilege of
> being the first man to discover *DIMENSION X*?

> BRAD
> Now I know why he's pushing us out.

> MIKE
> That's right—I want to steal all the credit.
> *(Cocks his ear to one side)*
> Listen to that music. Isn't it great? Go on.
> Honest, I'm a big boy now.

He shoos them both toward the door. They exit and Brad at the door turns.

> BRAD
> *(Looks at Helen, shrugs helplessly)*
> Well, call me if anything happens.
> *(Leaves)*

18. CLOSE-UP – MIKE

> MIKE
> *(Waves, smiles)*
> Have a good time!
> *(Pushes door closed and softly to himself)*
> Dance a set for me!

FADE-OUT:

FADE-IN:

19. INT. HELEN'S ROOM AT LODGE – NIGHT – MED. SHOT OF DOOR

The *SOUND* of a key in lock and the door opens to reveal a *BELLHOP* carrying the dresses and luggage. He comes in and Brad and Helen follow. The bellhop drapes the wardrobe over the bed, puts down the luggage, and starts to busy himself straightening the room. Helen surveys the room. It is done in excellent "Early American" with large leaded windows of stained glass.

> HELEN
> It's just beautiful, Brad.
> *(She kisses him)*
> Thank you.

> BRAD
> Don't thank me. Mike got it for you.

> HELEN
> Brad, why didn't you tell me about Mike?
> I mean, you know, his condition.

> BRAD
> I didn't think there was any need to. He's
> been an invalid all his life—polio. He accepts
> it the way some people are tall or short, thin or
> fat. Believe me, it doesn't bother him at all.

> HELEN
> I wonder. He's sure a wonderful person.
> I'm glad he likes me.

20.   CLOSE-UP – BELLHOP

The bellhop has just closed the window and walks into Helen and Brad.

> BELLHOP
> Anything else I can do, Doctor Curtis?

> BRAD
> Yes, would you confirm our reservation in
> the dining room for me?

He hands the bellhop two dollars.

                    BELLHOP
               (Smiling)
     Sorry, can't take any tips from you, sir.
     It's all been taken care of.

                     BRAD
     Mike?

                    BELLHOP
     Yes sir, he's paid for everything in advance—
     the dinner, champagne, the special cake, and
     those flowers.
               *(Points to a big bouquet on the dresser.
               Helen sees them for the first time, goes over,
               and fishes out a card.)*

21.   TWO-SHOT – BRAD AND BELLHOP

                     BRAD
     How do you like that character?

Helen walks over to Brad with the card.

                     HELEN
     Oh, Brad, he is so sweet to do all this. Listen,
     "To our girl" – signed Mike.

                    BELLHOP
     He's been here all day today, making
     sure everything was just right.

                     BRAD
               (Half to himself)
     No wonder he hadn't worked on the new
     equipment. He's been here all day.

                    BELLHOP
     Miss, I closed the window. We're expecting a storm.

HELEN
Fine, thank you very much.

BELLHOP
You're welcome, ma'am, well, happy wedding party!

Bellhop exits.

HELEN
Did Mike tell them it was a wedding celebration?

BRAD
Guess so, that's just like him. He won't wait for nothing. Speaking about waiting, we better get moving if they have a dinner for us.

Helen has selected a dress and moves to the next room.

HELEN
Just let me change into this dress and I'll be right with you, honey.

She goes into the next room, leaves the door half-ajar.

BRAD
All right.

Brad picks up the card and walks over to look at the flowers, sniffs at them.

BRAD
(To himself)
What a guy!

Helen calls from the next room.

HELEN
Brad?

BRAD
Yeah?

HELEN
What's Dimension "X"?

BRAD
What's what?

Helen comes out in a smart evening gown, comes to him and turns her back.

HELEN
Zip me. Dimension "X"—what is it?

BRAD
That's the project we've been working on for the last two years.

HELEN
I know that, silly. I mean, what is it, what does it do?

BRAD
(Laughs lightly)
It doesn't do anything. It's just a name we gave something. How come you're interested all of a sudden?

HELEN
(Zipped, turns)
Well, you said it was dangerous and I get to worrying about Mike.

She starts combing hair and putting on lipstick, etc.

BRAD
Well, it's not dangerous—that is, we don't know. It just might be, that's all.

HELEN
Maybe you should call him and tell him not
to fool with it tonight and wait for you!

BRAD
Are you serious? Honey, actually, Mike is my
superior in addition to being the best electronics
engineer/physicist in the country!

HELEN
He is?

BRAD
Of course, he's written half the manuals and
textbooks being used.

HELEN
He did?

BRAD
Sure. Did you see those two tubes and unites
we were talking about at the lab, the one for "X"?

HELEN
(Combing hair)
Yes.

BRAD
He's the one who worked out the basic diagram
for them and if it works, he might well be our next
Nobel Prize winner.

HELEN
Sounds exciting, what will this Dimension "X" be?

BRAD
Well, we don't know. That's why we call it "X."
"X" is the symbol meaning unknown, and with the

new equipment, we hope to penetrate a completely unknown area of radio frequencies never touched before.

                    HELEN
Sounds wonderful and complicated.

                    BRAD
Not really—look.

He holds his hands up, palms facing in about a foot apart.

                    BRAD
        (Continues, indicates left hand)
Now this point is the highest radio frequency we know about...
        (Now indicates other hand)
...and this point is the lowest LIGHT frequency we know of, but in between is an area that has never been discovered. It might be sound, light, or you name it.

She is ready now and she walks over to him—takes his hands in hers, she smiles cutely.

                    HELEN
All right! I'll name it—uh, Herman.

                    BRAD
Can't call a scientific thing like this Herman. It needs an unusual name like "X."

                    HELEN
Shows how much you know. "X" is a very common name where I come from.

                    BRAD
It is?

> HELEN
> Sure, every Hollywood divorcee has a former spouse they call their "EX."

> BRAD
> *(Breaks up)*
> Oh, you're a clever girl…

> HELEN
> …and a hungry one, let's go see what Mike prepared for you.

> BRAD
> *(Grabs her)*
> How about one little kiss first?

> HELEN
> *(Shocked)*
> But sir! We won't be married for six more weeks.

> BRAD
> One on account—C'mon.

She melts into his arms. They kiss.

> BRAD
> Whew!

> HELEN
> *(Leads him to the door by hand)*
> C'mon, let's go before I lose my appetite!

They laughingly go out the door as we…

FADE-OUT:

FADE-IN:

22.   INT. EXPERIMENTAL STATION – MED. SHOT – NIGHT

MOVE INTO C.U. Mike is over in the "workshop" section of the room. He is working with a screwdriver on one of two long pipes that stick up about two feet apart as large candle holders on top of a panel filled with dials, switches, etc.

He tightens this, then squints as he measures the other. Satisfied, he wipes his palms on his pants' legs, reaches under the bench, and brings up the two cardboard boxes holding the new tubes. He sets them on the bench and takes one out. It's carefully wrapped in excelsior paper. Gently, he blows at the flecks of dust on it, examines it with the pride of a connoisseur with a bottle of rare old brandy, decides it's all right, holds it up, and kisses it lightly.

>   MIKE
>   Be there, baby!

He reaches up and sets it into one of the large sockets. That done, he starts to unwrap the other when there is a flash of lightning and a low rumble of thunder. He looks up for a second and then continues with the tube. He's about to put it in the socket when a *BANGING NOISE* is *HEARD* offstage. He looks.

CUT TO:

23.   SHUTTERS FLAPPING INT.

A strong wind has started to blow up and some papers are blown off the table. With an air of disgust at the interruption, he carefully puts the tube down, wheels over, and closes the window. We *PAN BACK* with him and he continues where he left off. The tubes secured, he starts flicking a brace of switches. He checks the new power units, dusting them down with a cloth. He plugs in two large cables from it into the switchboard on the table. Now he checks a large decibels meter that has a large piece of tape pasted above the "peak" side of the meter that reads, Dimension "X."

24.   INSERT OF METER

Now, he flicks on the oscilloscope and checks on a wave on the round screen. It hums but is a straight line. Now, he's ready. A quick check of the dials and he turns to a power switch on the new units, pauses a moment nervously, then with a sudden surge of decision, pushes the lever into contact. There is a winding hum as the generators stir into action.

Now the new tubes begin to glow dimly. Quickly, he checks the levels on the oscilloscope and the DB meter – they are both inactive. He turns two dials gradually, checking the meters constantly. Now the hum gets louder, the tubes brighter. He checks the levels and starts to make quick notes in the logbook opened in front of him.

25.   CLOSE-UP OF PANEL WITH DB METER

We see Mike's hands move in and turn two dials next to the meter. Now we see the meter begin to rise, higher and higher the needle moves toward the area marked "X." Now the humming sound grows *LOUDER* and more piercing. We *PULL BACK* to a *MEDIUM SHOT* and see the excitement on his face. His brow is wet with the intensity of the moment. Feverishly, he makes notes in the logbook of the readings. He boosts the power again.

CUT TO:

26.   METER

The needle is wavering precariously close to "X"!

27.   MED. SHOT

Now he is completely obsessed with the nearness of the success they've waited for. He flicks some more switches, turns one dial very carefully. The *SOUND* rises higher, then suddenly changes in tune and rather than high in volume, it thins out into a flat sound like the rushing of wind! He looks up at the meter.

CUT TO:

28. INSERT METER

The needle is now wavering past the line that marks "X"!

CUT TO:

29. CLOSE-UP MIKE

He looks in almost disbelief! Then he almost jumps with exultation.

> MIKE
> It's in! It's in!

Now he turns another dial, but nothing moves. The meter holds at the same level inside "X." Now he picks up the logbook, puts it in his lap, and wheels his chair around to the desk. As he backs away from the table, he notices the two tubes above the rig on the table. His eyes widen in amazement! Around the two tubes and filling the entire two-foot, area between them is a multi-hued ring of bright color!

NOTE – Although this picture is shot in black and white, from this point on, *COLOR* objects will be superimposed on the black and white film. This unique combination should prove quite startling!

Mike stares at the ring of color for a moment and then turns his back to the console and wheels to the desk and picks up the phone.

> MIKE
> *(Into phone)*
> Dorothy, this is Mike! Get me Dr. Curtis. He's at the Inn. Hurry please, it's very important. What, he should be in the dining room. Please hurry.

While Mike is waiting for Brad to come to the phone, he reaches down in his lap and puts the logbook on the desk in front of him. He makes little entries interspersed with looks over his shoulder at the pulsating ring of color that now has enveloped the area all around the tubes, like a brilliant cloud. The loud rushing, whining *SOUND* that emanates from the equipment remains constant as he waits impatiently and he looks over to the large DB meter. It is still in the lower part of the "X" range.

30.   INSERT METER

Needle holding on "X."

31.   BACK TO MIKE AT DESK

Impatiently, he calls into phone.

                    MIKE
            Hello—HELLO!

No answer yet, he writes some more, holding the phone crooked between his shoulder and head.

CUT TO:

32.   INT. THE INN – NIGHT

Brad and Helen walk up to a brace of house phones on a shelf against a wall. Brad picks one up.

                    BRAD
            Hello. This is Doctor Curtis. You have a call
            for me, please.

Brad turns to Helen, laughing.

                    BRAD
            He's like a kid. He's gotta find out how we took
            the surprise.

                    HELEN
          Let me talk to him too. I want to thank him!

                    BRAD
               (Into phone)
          Hello, hello, you character. What's the idea
          spending all this money on us!

CUT TO:

33.   INT. CABIN – NIGHT
                    MIKE
               (Impatiently)
          Forget it—I didn't call about that. Brad, listen
          close. I put in the…

He's interrupted at the other end.

CUT TO:

34.   INT. INN – HOUSE PHONES

                    HELEN
               (Anxious to talk to him)
          Let me talk to him, honey.

Brad gives her the phone.

                    HELEN
               (Continues)
          Mike, you sweet, wonderful Santa Claus,
          you. You shouldn't have done it, but it was
          wonderful.

CUT TO:

35.   INT. CABIN—MIKE

                    MIKE
              (Impatient, but polite)
        My pleasure, Helen, but look, we'll talk
        about that later. Please put Brad on. I've got
        to tell him…

He is interrupted now by a brilliant *CRACK OF LIGHTNING*, the flash lights up the whole room!

CUT TO:

36.   INSERT OF LIGHTNING HITTING THEIR RADIO TOWER

The tower shakes from the impact.

CUT TO:

37.   INT. CABIN – MIKE – CLOSE-UP

He looks up sharply as it hits. He surveys the room quickly. Everything's all right so he turns back to the phone.

38.   ANOTHER ANGLE – MIKE

THE CAMERA PULLS BACK from back of Mike hunched over, talking on the phone and *TRUCKS* over to the meter. We *HEAR* Mike talking in the background.

We move in close on the meter and see it at the low point wavering, wavering, and then slowly, slowly it starts to rise! Steadily, now the needle climbs higher and higher and *HIGHER*, until now it is at the end of the meter and can go no higher! Slowly, the *CAMERA PULLS BACK* for a *WIDER ANGLE* that takes in the table, the equipment, and the entire wall area. As Mike talks, unaware of what is happening, we see the small cloud of pulsating color around the tubes take on a vaporous steaming appearance that starts to expand, to swirl and eddy like a multi-hued fog!

Larger the mass becomes until it covers the entire wall back of Mike! Now the fog disperses and seems to solidify into a translucent appearing membrane that seems to have replaced the wall of the room. Slowly as we watch this membrane, we seem to see "something" moving behind it.

Now slowly a pinpoint of smoke and a small hole starts to burn into the lower center portion of it. Larger and larger the hole burns (the same way a sheet of plastic will melt if you put heat to it), until it is a foot in diameter, two feet…three…Now we can see in, it is like a look into some strange, surrealistic world! We make out vague shapes of strangely colored trees, and hills all shimmering in a steaming fog-like atmosphere. It is incredible.

Now the form we saw moving behind it comes to the burned out opening and peers through into the room. It is a large *HUMAN FORM*, but there the resemblance ends. It has arms, legs, everything as we do, but it is a mass of steaming swirling *COLORS*. Its head has eyes that seem to be illuminated from within. Now it looks into the room almost curiously. Then it pulls itself bodily into the room and stands there with a look of someone who had entered a strange new world. For a moment, this steaming mass of color stands looking curiously.

      MIKE
    (Off stage)
Yes, yes, thank you, Helen, now please let me talk to Brad. Brad, listen, yes, I saw the lightning. I think it might have hit our tower. What? No, I don't think it hurt anything. Brad—will you please listen to me for a minute? We've done it! What? What do you think I'm talking about.
    (Laughs)
That's right! We've hit into it. It seems to have leveled off at the low point of the DB, but that's all right. All it means is that we have to boost the power output. Sure, then we can take it as HIGH as we want to go! Well, of course we start getting them built right away. Then who knows HOW far we can go!

>   *(Off stage)*
>   The main thing is, we broke through the barrier.
>   What? Yes, of course I'm logging everything.
>   Well, you can come over if you want to!

CUT TO:

39.   CLOSE-UP – MIKE

He's sweating.

>   MIKE
>   Well, I thought I'd let it run awhile to see how
>   it holds up, but it's generating a lot of heat now,
>   so I better shut it off. Don't want to burn it out now!

CUT TO:

40.   INT. INN – BRAD – CLOSE-UP

>   BRAD
>   *(On phone)*
>   No, that's all we need! I knew the function in
>   the tubes would do it.

CUT TO:

41.   INT. CABIN – MED. TWO-SHOT

Now we see Mike at phone in alcove and the creature standing behind by the hole from where he crawled out. The creature is standing there weaving back and forth as we amplify the whining sound of the equipment. This is the way the creature hears its high, penetrating…

42.   CLOSE-UP – THE CREATURE

He looks toward the area the sound is coming from. It obviously hurts his ears because he raises his hands and covers his ears. For a moment, he stands there weaving back and forth holding his head trying to block out the sound. His face becomes contorted in a frightening expression of agony and his mouth opens as if to scream in pain, but no sound comes out!

CUT TO:

43. BACK TO MIKE

> MIKE
> The tubes—I almost forgot! Brad, the weirdest thing, the tubes and the whole area around them is covered in a steaming cloud of color. That's right—all the colors of the rainbow! The brightest hues I've ever seen. "X" must cut into the color spectrum somewhere between where sound ends and light begins.

CUT TO:

44. MED. SHOT THE CREATURE

Holding his ears, he weaves belabored toward the equipment and smashes at it, flailing his arms in wide pushing motions. The speakers and transmitter are smashed to the floor.

CUT TO:

45. CLOSE-UP – MIKE

Mike turns from the phone at the sound of the equipment being broken. He wheels his chair around and then he sees the creature. He stares in disbelief – unable to move, rigid with an uncomprehending fear! Then he hears Brad at the other end of the phone.

> BRAD
> *(Filter)*
> Mike…Mike! You there, Mike?

Mike hears the voice and it shakes him out of the trance.

>   MIKE
>   *(Intense, trying to be factual)*
>   Brad. Listen close and listen quick, I don't know
>   what it is, but the lightning boosted X to the
>   top and there's a huge monster here. No,
>   listen to me. He's a multicolored giant, a demon!
>   He steams a polychromatic aura all around him.
>   He's a maze of brilliant colors, all different colors.

46.   MIKE AND CREATURE

47.   POV MIKE

The Demon turns toward Mike and stares a moment, then starts to lumber toward him.

>   MIKE
>   *(Continues)*
>   He's coming toward me, Brad. He's a
>   demon from some other world. He stepped
>   right through a wall here in the cabin. He
>   radiates a tremendous pulsating heat. We
>   did it, Brad. We brought him in through
>   Dimension X. He's coming for me. He's
>   coming closer. He's white hot. Brad, he's
>   coming right at me. He's...he's...

48.   CLOSE-UP – MIKE

Filled with terror, Mike stares at it coming to him. He starts to SCREAM wildly. Scream after scream and then he is covered with a multicolored blanket of heat as the monster hovers over him. Mike is now like a man who is in an electric chair. He strains taut. His jacket starts to smoke in spots.

He straightens up as though to get out of the chair and then, like a puppet with the strings cut, falls back into a smoldering heap, the phone receiver dangling from the end of the cord, as his lifeless fingers release it. From the phone, we HEAR Brad on the other end…"Mike…Mike. Are you all right, Mike?"

We see Mike lying there slumped on the floor and now the color that covered him pulls back as the creature moves away.

CUT TO:

49.   THE CREATURE

Turns back to the equipment, gives a last, angry swipe at it, and the *SOUND* is stilled. It turns not to the membranous wall it came through and from his POV, we see the melted opening in the membrane start to heal up and close. It is gone and now the steaming polychromatic cloud starts to disappear.

CUT TO:

50.   CLOSE-UP – THE DEMON

A look of disbelief and confusion covers his face.

CUT TO:

51.   MED. SHOT DEMON

He rushes forth into the cloud trying to find the *HOLE*, but it is gone and just a small vaporous cloud is all that remains. Now that disappears and the wall of the cabin reappears as it was. The creature looks around helplessly. He is trapped in another world. A world that is frightening to him, a strange hell that has *NOISE*—penetrating, agonizing noise.

The creature stands there, his steaming, multicolored body pulsating as though he were thinking. Then his color becomes brighter, almost blindingly light and he pushes wildly at the wall where the window is, and burning, and breaking through sheer strength, rips half the wall out, and disappears into the night, like a spent meteor tailing its way into a dark eternity.

FADE-OUT:

FADE-IN:

52.   INT. CABIN – LATER THAT NIGHT—CLOSE-UP

The cabin is a shambles. A large, fat man is kneeling over Mike's body. He is *SHERIFF WALT KEMMER*. He pushes his short brimmed Stetson back onto his head and scratches at the bald spot as he squints appraisingly. He slowly chews the stub of a toothpick lodged in the corner of a fat florid face. Wheezing, he gets to his feet and the *CAMERA PULLS BACK* to reveal Brad comforting Helen to one side while standing next to the Sheriff is his *DEPUTY*, a thin, lanky man with a bland, leathery face.

>   DEPUTY
>   *(Flatly)*
>   What d'ya think, Sheriff?

>   SHERIFF
>   I don't know. He's been burned, that's fer sure.

He ambles around the room, walks over to the big hole in the wall, looks at it for a moment, and then walks over to the workbench and looks at the equipment scattered all over. He picks at this, pokes at that, grunts to himself, and walks over to Brad and Helen.

>   SHERIFF
>   Well, whatever it was did it, sure made a mess
>   of the place.

Brad looks up and nods.

>   BRAD
>   Yeah.
>   *(To Helen)*
>   You all right, honey?

>   HELEN
>   *(Dabs at eyes and nods)*

I think so. Oh, Brad. Poor Mike!

She sneaks a look over at the body. Another flood of tears takes over and she buries her head in Brad's shoulder. He comforts her.

> BRAD
> I know.
> *(Shudders)*

The Sheriff calls to the Deputy.

> SHERIFF
> Sill, throw a blanket or somethin' over that.

The Deputy nods and takes a blanket off the back of the couch and drapes it over the still form.

> SHERIFF
> *(Looking to bench)*
> I always wondered what you fellas had
> goin' on in this place. Looks like some kind of
> a radio station—that what it is?

> BRAD
> In a way.
> *(Sees how upset Helen is)*
> Why don't you go out and wait in the car?
> We'll just be a few minutes.

> HELEN
> No, I want to stay with you…please!

> BRAD
> All right, then sit over here.

Takes her to an easy chair, notices it faces Mike's body so he turns it so it faces away. Gently eases her into it. Brad now walks over to equipment to appraise the damage—Sheriff follows.

SHERIFF
Got any ideas what done it?

BRAD
(Hedging)
Not really.

SHERIFF
He didn't die no natural death that's fer sure. He's been electrocuted, wouldn't you say?

BRAD
Yes, I would.

SHERIFF
(Squints)
We had a big bolt of lightning hit, think that did it?

BRAD
Yes, I do.

SHERIFF
Funny, you told me earlier you was on the phone with him when it struck.

BRAD
Did I? I don't remember.

SHERIFF
Well I do. Look, if you got any notion about who done it, you better talk up 'cause from where I sit, you could've very easy done it.

Helen jumps up and goes to Brad, then faces the Sheriff.

HELEN
(Heated)
How dare you talk that way, Dr. Curtis is one

of our most respected scientists.

SHERIFF

He's still a human being, ma'am, and I seen human beings pull some strange things, no matter what kind a fancy label they had.

HELEN

Besides, Dr. Curtis was with me at the Inn when it happened.

SHERIFF

Look, ma'am, I ain't sayin' he done it, but I kinda get the feelin' he knows who did.

HELEN

Brad, you don't know anything about all of this, do you?
    (Brad just stands)
Brad, why won't you answer?

BRAD

He wouldn't believe me.

SHERIFF

Try me, mister.

HELEN

Please Brad, tell him.

BRAD

(Flatly)
All right. He was killed by a monster from another world.

The Sheriff and the Deputy and Helen all gather close with amazed stares on their faces.

                SHERIFF
He was what?

                BRAD
I'm repeating what Mike told me was going on when he was killed. There was a monster in the room with him.

The Sheriff breaks into laughter and followed by the Deputy.

                SHERIFF
You expect me to believe that—a monster!
                (Laughs)

                BRAD
        (Calmly)
No, I don't expect you to, I only know what Mike told me. A multi-hued demon, he called it, from another world, came into the room. It was white hot, he said.

                SHERIFF
Came into the room how? The doors locked from the inside, you had the key.

                BRAD
What about the hole in the wall?

They walk over there.

                SHERIFF
Nothing came in this way. his wall has been pushed out by somethin' real strong though, but it weren't no monster.

Deputy points to scorched mark.

DEPUTY
What's that, Sheriff?

SHERIFF
Looks like a large hand print burned right into the wood. A human-appearing hand print but what could generate enough heat to burn into wood.
(Walks to table)
This equipment was practically melted. It don't make sense.

BRAD
Unless it was a fiery being, like Mike said.

SHERIFF
(Looks straight at Brad, finally shakes his head)
Huh!
(Walks back to bench)
These are pretty powerful generators. They could melt this, couldn't they?

BRAD
Not unless they burned themselves out, and these tubes with it, and you'll notice they are still intact. No, Mike said the demon generated intense heat and that could have caused this.

HELEN
(To Brad)
But Brad, it's so unbelievable—a monster! It sounds like those horror things I do in Hollywood.

BRAD
I know it. I find it hard to believe myself, but Mike was so calm when he described everything as it happened, in detail. What the monster

looked like, where it came from…

                SHERIFF
Where did it come from?

                BRAD
                (Hesitates)
Well, I don't know exactly, but it has to do with this.

Brad indicates the BD meter.

53.   INSERT METER

It is scorched except for a white line at the top.

                BRAD
Notice that white line. That is where the needle was when this was exposed to intense heat.

                HELEN
It's all the way into Dimension X!

                SHERIFF
What's Dimension X?

                BRAD
I'm sorry, Sheriff, I'm not at liberty to discuss that.

                SHERIFF
What do you mean, not at liberty?

                BRAD
It's a secret project. I can't talk about it.

                SHERIFF
           (Jerks a thumb to Mike's body)
Well, neither can he, and I'm gonna find out why.

> BRAD
> I've told all I know.

> SHERIFF
> *(Mad)*
> I know what you tol' me—you don't think I
> SWALLOW A COCK 'N BULL STORY about
> demons, do ya? But, you're right about one
> thing, this machine, whatever it is, had somethin'
> to do with killin' him and I'm gonna find out who's
> responsible, secret or not!

Helen looks at the body and starts to cry softly.

> BRAD
> Sheriff, Mike was our closest friend—believe me.
> I am as anxious to straighten this out as you are,
> but I don't have the answers yet. I would like to
> get Miss Terry out of here now. If we're free to go…

> SHERIFF
> *(Resigned)*
> I'm not holding you, go on, but you be back
> here 10 o'clock this morning.

> BRAD
> For what?

> SHERIFF
> For the inquest, I wanta see the Coroner's face
> when you tell him what done it.

The Sheriff starts for the door with the Deputy following…Brad stops the Deputy.

> BRAD
> *(Indicates Mike's body)*
> You're not going to leave him like that!

Deputy smiles a snaggle-toothed grin.

> DEPUTY
> Why not…he ain't goin' no place.

Turns and goes out the door.

CUT TO:

54.   EXT. CABIN—NIGHT

Deputy and Sheriff get into Sheriff's car. The Sheriff snorts sarcastically, as he opens the door.

> SHERIFF
> Demons! Monsters…who's he think he's kiddin'?

The car pulls away and we see Helen and Brad standing outside the door.

> HELEN
> Oh Brad, it's all so…

> BRAD
> …unbelievable? Helen, don't you believe I'm telling the truth?

> HELEN
> Yes, I believe you are telling the truth, as far as you know it, but isn't it possible that Mike might've been…

> BRAD
> (Interrupts)
> Look, honey, Mike was a cold, calculating scientist, not given to exaggerations or hallucinations. He described it in detail and that mess in there was caused by "something."

                    HELEN
I'm sorry, darling. Of course, you're right,
but what are you going to do? The Sheriff
doesn't believe you!

                    BRAD
I don't know, but as crazy or fantastic as it
seems, I intend to proceed on the premise
that a "monster" does exist, because if he
does, it's roaming around loose somewhere
and could strike again!

Brad takes Helen by the arm and they head across the open area toward their car. As they cross over, we see a multi-hued shape dimly glowing in the distance, half hidden by the woods, pulsating…pulsating.

FADE-OUT:

FADE-IN:

55.   INT. CABIN – DAY

It's the next morning. Two attendants are carrying Mike's body out on a stretcher. The *CORONER* is making notes in a book as the Sheriff and Deputy stands watching him, as Brad comes through the door alone.

                    SHERIFF
Where's your young lady?

                    BRAD
I let her stay at the Inn. You don't need her,
do you?

                    SHERIFF
No, guess not.

Turns to Coroner, a slight, dried-up old man.

SHERIFF
(Continues)
Doc! This is the fella that worked with the victim—name's Curtis.

CORONER
(Scowls)
You gonna pay fer the deceased?

BRAD
(Taken aback)
What?

CORONER
Someone has to sign fer funeral expenses.

SHERIFF
The Doc's also the local mortician. He'll lay your friend out real good.

BRAD
(Sick at this cold-bloodedness)
Yes, I'll be responsible for all expenses!

CORONER
(Relieved smile)
Good, ain't in business fer my health, ya understand.

DEPUTY
Tell him what ya tol' us Curtis, about what killed yer friend. Go on, ya know.

CORONER
(Squints over glasses)
Oh, this the one that seen a "monster"?

BRAD
(Patiently)
I didn't say I saw anything!

CORONER
(Laughs)
Look, you don't have to dream up no stories, son. I tol' the Sheriff it was "accidental death due to electrocution" and that's how my Coroner's report reads. You're in the clear!

BRAD
He was electrocuted, then?

CORONER
He was burned and shocked—both. That bolt a lightning sure was a strong one.

SHERIFF
We knew that's what done it 'cause a flock a animals in a barn was burned on the other side of the hill last night. Doc says the animals was electrocuted same way yer friend was. Same bolt musta struck there too!

BRAD
Sheriff, don't you understand what this means? That creature killed the animals—NOT lightning! Besides, I've told you, I was on the phone with Mike when that lightning hit.

SHERIFF
S'matter with you? Trying to get yourself in trouble? Why don't ya quit while you're ahead? You keep talkin' like that and you're gonna scare a lotta folks outta their wits around here. Now forget it.

                        BRAD
                     (Impatient)
      I'm not trying to scare anyone. I'm trying to
      warn you. We've got to do something NOW
      before someone else is killed.

                      CORONER
                   (Slight chuckle)
      Well, I'm gonna do somethin' about it, son,
      an' I suggest you do the same. I'm goin'
      home an' take a nice, hot Saturday bath.

The Coroner starts packing his gear to leave and the phone RINGS.
The Deputy answers it.

                      CORONER
                     (Continues)
      Mind if I ride back into town with you, Walt?

                       DEPUTY
                      (On phone)
      Yeah, he's still here. Where? On the
      North road. Right, we'll be right over!

Deputy walks over to Sheriff, Coroner, and Brad.

                       SHERIFF
      What was that about?

                       DEPUTY
      Looks like our scientist friend here might
      have somethin' after all, Sheriff.

                       SHERIFF
      What d'ya mean?

                       DEPUTY
      Seems like a lightnin' bolt struck and killed

a guy about ten minutes ago. Huh, and
there ain't a cloud in the sky!

They look at each other as we...

FADE-OUT:

FADE-IN:

56.   EXT. – NORTH ROAD – DAY

We see a Forest Ranger truck and the Sheriff's car parked off to the side of a deserted stretch of road. On the road itself, two *FOREST RANGERS* and the Sheriff are gathered near an old car that has cheap suitcases and cardboard boxes strapped with rope across the top. The hood is up and the car is still smoking slightly.

We move in for a *MEDIUM SHOT* of the Rangers and Sheriff at the front of the car, and notice a blanket draped over a still form lying half-sprawled across the front bumper.

                    RANGER 1
That's how we found 'em Sheriff. He was still smokin' when we got here.

                    SHERIFF
            (Peeking under blanket)
He's been burned crisp, ain't he?

                    RANGER 2
We figure the motor caught fire while he was fixin' it. See there.
            (Points to fender)

Fender's melted.

                    SHERIFF
Yeah, but the motor ain't burned hardly at all.

How'd ya find this anyway?

                RANGER 1

Mountain lookout saw it. Says he seen a bright flash of colors just like the rainbow, flashed up real bright. He thought it was a fire startin' but it was all kinds of colors, couldn't figure it out. So, we came down to take a look and found him like this...
     (Nods to blanket)
...and her just the way she is.

The Ranger points over to a tree and the *CAMERA PANS* to:

57.   GROUP SHOT

Coroner, Brad, and Deputy are around a plain-looking flaxen-haired girl of 20 who sits wide-eyed and staring against the tree. She has a completely blank expression. Near her are a checked tablecloth and all the fixings for what looks like a picnic lunch. The Coroner is bent over and examining her. She doesn't move. He straightens up.

                CORONER
She's in shock all right.

                DEPUTY
Think she'll come out of it, Doc?

                CORONER
Hard to say, guess she will in time.
Right now, she should have some rest.

Sheriff and one of the Rangers walk over.

                SHERIFF
     (To Brad)
Same kind a burns your friend got. Mind, I ain't sayin' it was a monster done it, but

it sure wasn't no lightning this time! How's she?
(Brad shrugs)
(Sheriff nods to girl)
What ya think, Doc?

CORONER
She ain't moved a muscle. We had better move her somewhere she can get some sleep. I can give her a sedative—might bring her out of it.

SHERIFF
Nearest hospital is down in the city, take a good hour ana half.

CORONER
Too far, trip'll do her more harm than good. She really shouldn't be moved at all.

DEPUTY
It's only three miles up to the Inn.

BRAD
My financee has a room there. If you'd like, we can keep her there.

Sheriff looks at the Coroner.

CORONER
That'd be better—nice and quiet.

SHERIFF
Okay, C'mon. Sill, let's get the lady on her feet.

They carefully pick her up and take her to the Sheriff's car. As they walk, the Deputy talks. The girl's face in *CLOSE-UP* facing the sun.

                        DEPUTY
    Somethin' sure scared the daylights outta her!
    Wonder what coulda done it.

The *CAMERA PANS UP* from them and to the bright sun cross-fading down to another angle on the far side of the hill. here we see the demon standing spraddle-legged, arms outstretched with its face up into the sun drinking in its bright rays. Its steaming colors pulsating… pulsating…pulsating!

FADE-OUT:

FADE-IN:

58.   INT. HELEN'S ROOM AT INN—AFTERNOON

The shades are drawn and lying on the bed is the shock victim, her eyes are closed now. She is asleep. Brad and Helen are watching her from across the room. Now the girl stirs, and whimpers in her sleep—a soft sobbing sound.

                        HELEN
                  (Sympathetically)
    Poor kid!

                        BRAD
    Yeah, they had to travel half way across
    the country to end up like this!

                        HELEN
    Brad, you think the demon did this?

                        BRAD
    Well, it wasn't an accident or lightning.
                  (Looks at watch)
    She's been asleep three hours.

                    HELEN
Think she'll be able to talk when she wakens?

                    BRAD
I hope so. She'll be able to clear alotta things up.
          (Impatiently)
Can't figure out what's keeping Myers.

                    HELEN
Who?

                    BRAD
Dr. Myers from the University, I called him
this morning. He's the head of our psychic
research department.

                    HELEN
What's that?

                    BRAD
Oh, they investigate all unusual things, like
mental telepathy, ESP, Retrogression through
hypnosis…even ghosts.
          (Slight laugh)
He's one man I know who won't think this demon
doesn't exist!

                    HELEN
Brad, I thought scientists deal with facts!

                    BRAD
We do and it becomes more apparent to
scientists the further we probe into life and
its secrets, that anything is possible.

There is a slight *KNOCK* at the door and the Deputy sticks his head in, nods to Brad.

                    DEPUTY
                   (Whispers)
         There's a couple a fellers out here to see ya.
         Should I let 'em in?

                    BRAD
         No, I'll come out.

Helen nods toward the girl in bed.

                    HELEN
         I'll stay with her.

CAMERA FOLLOWS Brad to the door.

CUT TO:

59.   INT. HELEN'S HALLWAY

A short, middle-aged man, *DOCTOR IRA MYERS*, and a clean-cut man of 35, are waiting as Brad comes out the door. Brad grasps the hand of the short man warmly.

                    BRAD
         Oh, Ira. Do I need you!

                    MYERS
         I'd have been here sooner but I had to wait for
         Jim Hunter here Jim, say hello to Brad Curtis.

They exchange ad-libs.

                    HUNTER
         Sorry I held things up, but I had to get special
         orders cut from Washington.

                    BRAD
         Washington? I don't get it.

MYERS
Jim is a SPECIAL Agent assigned to investigate this situation. We might need some legal force if it gets out of hand.

BRAD
You're so right. I can't get anybody around here to believe me enough to do anything about it.

HUNTER
Can't blame them. It's pretty fantastic. The way it's been explained to me.

BRAD
Then you don't believe this monster exists?

HUNTER
Sir, let's say I don't disbelieve it either...if scientists of your reputation say it's so, then we'll go along and be safe!

BRAD
(Sighs relief)
That's good enough. I think when the girl in there is able to talk, she'll verify what Mike described he saw.

MYERS
Of course, I am completely fascinated by your demon, as you call him. He could give us the answer of what to expect when we make our first trip through space to another planet, which is not too far off!

BRAD
If anyone can get close enough to him without being burned to death.

                    MYERS
That brings up an interesting point. The young
lady in there…If your demon was responsible for
the car incident, and she was there, why wasn't
she electrocuted also?

                    BRAD
               (Shrugs)
        I don't know but…

Brad is interrupted by a *LOUD SCREAM* and sobbing from the room.

                    BRAD
We may get our answers in a moment!
        *(Brad quickly opens the door
        and they walk in)*

CUT TO:

60.   INT. HELEN'S ROOM

As they come in the door, the blond girl is sitting up straight in the bed. She is wide-eyed with terror, sobbing and staring at the far wall. Helen has run over to her and is trying to comfort her but she just stares. Dr. Myers goes over to her.

                    MYERS
             (Comforting)
    It's all right, my dear, you're safe now.

She just stares at the wall. Dr. Myers looks over and sees what is frightening her…The sun filtering through the partly drawn drapes is coming through a crest of strained glass in the English-lodge-type window…It's throwing an enlarged multicolored pattern on the wall!

                    MYERS
        Pull the drapes tight, quick!

Hunter does, and the reflection disappears. The girl now seems to calm down a little.

>   MYERS
>   (Soothing)
>   There, see? It's all right. Nothing is going to
>   hurt you. My name is Myers, I'm a doctor and
>   I want to help you.

She's calmer but still no reaction.

>   MYERS
>   Do you hear me? Hmmm?
>   (No reaction)
>   You don't have to talk if you don't want to, just
>   nod your head, all right?

No reaction, she just stares. Myers looks up at the group in back of him and shakes his head. He looks back at her, and then takes her hand in his and strokes it gently. Brad leans over to Myers.

>   BRAD
>   Think she'll come out of it?

>   MYERS
>   I think so, that reflection on the wall frightened
>   her but it reminded her of something. so she
>   obviously hasn't lost her memory.

As Myers talks he has taken a pencil flashlight out of his pocket and trains it on her eyes…she stares unflinchingly.

>   MYERS
>   (To Brad)
>   Know who she is?

>   BRAD
>   Yes, the Sheriff went through their belongings.

They were just married last week in Oklahoma
City. Name's McCord, Betty Ann, and his was Willis.

      MYERS

Good.
  (Turns back to her)
Betty Ann? Betty, I am going to ask you some
questions, all right?
  (No response)
Try to answer if you can.
  (He shines the light in her eyes again)
You were married last week in Oklahoma. You're
now Mrs. McCord, remember? Betty Ann
McCord—isn't that wonderful?

To this, a slight smile crosses her lips. Although she still doesn't move, Dr. Myers sees this and becomes encouraged. They've struck a responsive note somewhere—he pursues it.

      MYERS

Yes, that's better. Was it a church wedding?
  (She moves her mouth slightly, but nothing
  comes out)
  (Gently)
I see, were you and Willis childhood sweethearts
before you were married?
  (She moves her lips again, and this time a
  faint but audible)

      BETTY

Oh…ye-ees.

      MYERS

(Cagey)
You were born in Missouri, didn't you tell me?
  (Now a faint frown crosses her brow—her
  mouth moves silently)

                    MYERS
        What? I can't hear you. What did you say?

                    BETTY
        I was born in Okl...la-ho...
              (She trails off)

                    MYERS
              (Pleasantly)
        Oh, yes, that's right, Oklahoma—I forgot.
              (Turns to Brad and the others,
              whispers)

                    MYERS
              (Whispering)
        Here goes.
              (Shines light at her)
        Betty Ann, the car is all packed and you're in
        California. You're on a dirt road leading up to
        the mountains.

Her face clouds up.

                    MYERS
        What happened, Betty Ann? You remember!
        What happened on that road in the mountains?
              (Her face clouds up even more and she
              starts to speak)

                    BETTY ANN
        We're going to live at Uncle...

As she speaks, we see the pencil light from her POV. The light wavers, shimmers, and grows brighter and brighter as we dissolve into a diffused dream-type sequence.

The entire sequence is played *WITHOUT* dialogue, and all we *HEAR* throughout is a musical surrealistic *SOUND*, which as the scene progresses will be augmented with an exaggerated form of the natural sounds that would occur. The entire sequence will be shot through glass that is all diffused except for a small area in the center that will photograph clear.

61.   EXT. NORTH ROAD—DAY

An old car piled with cardboard cartons on top, comes into the scene and has a blowout and limps to a stop…The boy and girl get out. She stretches happily although the boy looks at the tire disgusted. She kisses him, waves to the beautiful countryside and asks him if he's hungry. He is, so she reaches in and takes a blanket and pillows from the car and spreads them out under a large tree at the side of the road. She calls to him, he nods and turns on the radio (Now we *HEAR* a pop tune blaring in accompaniment to the basic dream sound).

62.   EXT. SIDE OF HILL—DAY

The demon is standing facing the sun, its arms and legs out-stretched. It is absorbing its rays as though it were its life-giving substance. At the *SOUND* of the brassy radio music, it stops and looks to the crest of the hill where the music is coming from, and curiously goes in that direction

CUT TO:

63.   SCENE FROM CAR

The boy is busy with the jack when she happily calls to him to get something for her.

In mock exasperation, he drops the jack, gets into the front seat, and reaches into the back to take out a large wicker basket. As he does so, he accidentally sits on the horn. It sticks and keeps bleating! Now it has joined the cacophony of sound. Peeved, the boy goes to the hood and lifts it.

CUT TO:

64.   DEMON ON HILL

He hears the car horn and a look of excruciating pain rips his face. His steaming multicolored face registers unbearable torture and he puts his hands up over his ears to drown out the sound. He weaves and writhes with pain, and then starts a laborious rocking walk toward the source of the noise—the car!

CUT TO:

65.   BOY AT THE CAR

The boy has his head under the hood trying to find a way of stopping the horn…he senses someone behind him, straightens up, and turns. Slowly, his eyes grow large in fright and amazement! From the demon's POV we get closer and closer to the boy. He stands there unable to move, pressing himself against the front of the car. Slowly a swirling mass of colors creep over him! is clothes start to smoke in different spots. He straightens up tautly for a moment, than falls back onto the front of the car—lifeless! Now the demon smashes at the car motor…the *SOUND STOPS*. We…

CUT TO:

66.   THE GIRL – CLOSE-UP

She has been watching this action transfixed. Now she finds a release and *SCREAMS* and *SCREAMS*!

CUT TO:

67.   THE DEMON

Reacts and turns.

CUT TO:

68.   THE GIRL

Wide-eyed, she registers the approach of the demon. Now she just stares for a moment. Her eyes roll up and she collapses. Our effect to show her unconsciousness is a swirling into an abysmal blackness.

In the black, the MUSIC diminishes and *CROSSFADES INTO* the sound of soft sobbing and we return to reality and the present, in:

69.   INT—HELEN'S ROOM—DAY

The girl, Betty Ann, is sobbing. Helen is sitting on the bed with her arm around her. Dr. Myers sighs, gets up from the chair, goes to the window, and opens it.

>   MYERS
>   Then what?
>
>   BETTY ANN
>   That's all I remember.
>   *(Sobs)*
>
>   HELEN
>   You'll be all right, Betty Ann, poor kid.
>
>   BETTY ANN
>   I stood there watchin' Willis. He couldn't move,
>   I couldn't either. I just stood there, watchin'
>   that horrible thing kill my Willis!
>
>   HELEN
>   We know. Now try to forget it for a little while
>   and get some rest, hmmm?
>
>   BETTY ANN
>   *(Sees them watching her)*
>   You believe me, don't you? You don't think I could
>   be tellin' a story, do you? That fiery thing was so
>   real! I swear it was.
>
>   HELEN
>   Sh…Sh…we believe you.

BRAD
(Aside)
Do you believe it, Mr. Hunter?

HUNTER
(Grim)
Yes sir, I sure do.

MYERS
There's no doubt of its existence now, is there?

BRAD
No, but what do we do about it?

MYERS
Well, if possible, we should try to determine its origin, its substance, and habits and so forth. This could be the most enlightening scientific discovery of all time.

JIM
That's true, Doctor, but I think we better consider public safety before anything. It's killed two people already.

BRAD
He's right, Ira, it's more of a menace than a scientific curiosity! At any rate, I don't think we should discuss it here. Let's go to my laboratory, that's where it all started...Maybe we can find something to go on there!

JIM
Well, you go on ahead. I'll meet you there. I'm gonna get all the manpower I can to close off this mountain area, so it can't get out.
*(They get set to go.
Brad turns to Helen)*

                    BRAD
            You'll stay with her, huh?
                    (She nods. He smiles and they go
                    out the door as one)

70.   INT. LABORATORY – LATE AFTERNOON

Brad is working with the equipment getting it cleaned up, and straightened out. Dr. Myers is leaning against the bench as Brad works; he is leafing through his logbooks.

                    MYERS
            Amazing, amazing, absolutely amazing! Boy,
            there's no doubt about it, Brad. The ultra high
            frequency of yours is responsible for that demon.

                    BRAD
            You mean, you think it created the monster?

                    MYERS
            No. It was probably more like opening a door
            that it merely walked through into our plane
            of existence.
                    (Brad tightens a bolt here, replaces an
                    electrical devise there as he talks)

                    BRAD
            But where did it come from? Mars, the moon,
            did it travel on light waves to earth, that's what
            has me stopped.

                    MYERS
            No, I don't think he is a visitor from outer space
            at all. Now this is purely theory, but it is something
            philosophers, psychics, and scientists have toyed
            with for centuries. It might be he is from right here
            on earth!

BRAD
What?

MYERS
Have you ever had the feeling that you were being watched? I mean when you knew there wasn't anyone else near you, or the feeling we get entering a strange place, and yet we feel we have been there before!

BRAD
Yes, I think we've all experienced that!

MYERS
Well, that's the basis of this theory! That's right here on earth, on our world, a complete civilization exists that we have felt, but have never seen, because it is on another plane, another vibration than ours! It's like your different radio broadcasts all being transmitted at the same time, yet they never cross each other, except occasionally during an electrical storm or the like.

BRAD
Yes, at which time we might get two different broadcasts on the same frequency or television. Local shows that are meant to telecast in perhaps a hundred-mile radius have been seen thousands of miles away due to electrical disturbances from storms!

MYERS
That's right, and when the lightening struck the other night it must have done the same thing. It crossed the two phases of life on this planet and opened the door that separated them just long enough for this creature to pass from one to the other.

BRAD
Then he's more or less trapped here, with
no way to get back to his own plane or vibration!

MYERS
It looks that way, unless we can reopen the
door for him!
(Brad nods to equipment)

BRAD
You mean with his?

MYERS
Why not, that's how he got here!

BRAD
(Enthused)
Yeah, if we could duplicate the energy that
lightning bolt boosted the power with, it might
work! I'd need an auxiliary generator to
supplement what we've got here to make it.

MYERS
I'll have Jim get us one from the Air Base in
Jepson right away.
*(Brad gives equipment a final check,
turns a switch, and the thing starts
to hum)*

BRAD
There, it works all right. Our monster just
destroyed the amplifier setup. I could use
a new one, but it isn't necessary to run it!
You know, that's a funny thing too. It melted
the amplifier here, and destroyed the car.
In both cases, it went after sound, didn't it?

MYERS
I'd thought about that too, also what the girl had said about the demon weaving and holding its ears! I think it's affected by sound, that the sounds that we've become accustomed to and take for granted are causing it pain! That's why the car incident and this could account for the animals being burned! The animals were frightened by it, they made noise and it killed them.

BRAD
Then any noise could very well set it off on another killing rampage?

MYERS
It seems logical. As far as we know, there is no sound in the rest of the universe, but here, it's affecting him like a dog hearing a high pitched siren!

BRAD
Then in his own sphere or vibration he might be a perfectly normal person, but here, the noises turn him into a murdering MADMAN!

MYERS
Yes, that could account for his actions, but the description of his appearance puzzles me.

BRAD
Well, he has a human form, ears and eyes.

MYERS
Yes, but why is he a polychromatic rainbow of colors?

                    BRAD
Well, you answered that yourself. If he is
on another vibration, and can't be seen,
his world probably absorbs different light
rays than we do, and the ones we see on
him are refracted lights. It could be, too,
that we look multicolored to him the way he
does to us!

                    MYERS
              (Absorbing it, sighs)
Yes, you know, I can't help but feel sorry for
that poor lost creature.

The *SOUND* of a car coming to a stop outside…Brad turns off the switch to the VHF.

                    BRAD
That's probably Hunter.

The door opens and Jim Hunter and a uniformed *STATE TROOPER* enters.

                    HUNTER
Well, we've got the entire area closed off
with armed Troopers! Uh, Captain Walker,
this is Dr. Myers and Dr. Curtis.
              (Ad lib Hellos)

                    CAPTAIN
Sir, what about the residents here, should we
have them evacuated?

                    JIM
There's no sense in creating a panic. Besides,
there isn't time. I think the most important thing
right now is to locate the monster and to try to
destroy it as soon as possible.

CAPTAIN

(Still can't believe it)

Monster! You know, if I didn't know who I was dealing with, I'd say you were all crazy. My men sure think I am! I had a heck of a time trying to explain what we were after.

MYERS

(Smiles slightly)

I know it is unbelievable, but I think, gentlemen, that our first step should be to locate it and try to communicate with it. It is possible we are dealing with an intelligent being that can be reasoned with!

CAPTAIN

But it's a killer, isn't it?

MYERS

Again, not without reason. We believe it kills because it can't tolerate noise of any kind. It's never heard our kind of noise before!

JIM

That may be so, but I think we should find it first and try to isolate it so it can't do any more damage.

CAPTAIN

Well, it won't get out of these hills, that's for sure, and our radio units are all in close contact so we'll know the first time he shows up. He should be easy to see in the dark if he glows like you say!

MYERS

Oh Jim, before we do anything, we need some supplies and a powerful generator right away.

Can you get them?

                    JIM
Just name it, sir.

Brad goes to desk with Jim

                    BRAD
Here, I'll write down the specifics for you.

CUT TO:

71.   TWO-SHOT – MEYERS AND CAPTAIN

                    CAPTAIN
                   (Disturbed)
Dr. Myers, if you want to talk to that thing, my men are combing the hills, and soon as they find it, we can go and see it face-to-face if you want.

                    MYERS
Excellent, Captain.

                    CAPTAIN
But sir, it would be a lot easier if we just destroyed it!

                    MYERS
                   (Solemn)
I'm not so sure, Captain.

                    CAPTAIN
What do you mean?

                    MYERS
It may be easier to talk to it than to destroy it… because I don't think it can be destroyed!

SLOW DISSOLVE:

72.   EXT. DESERTED ROAD – NIGHT

A state trooper's car grinds to a halt on the road, and we see two troopers get out and look down the edge of the hill into the darkness below. They see nothing, get back into the car, and check in on the radio.

CUT TO:

73.   INT. TROOPER CAR – NIGHT

                    TROOPER 1
          Trooper unit 11...trooper unit 11 to HQ
          operation Firefly—over.

                    CAPTAIN
              (Filter)
          This is Headquarters Operation Firefly,
          come in Unit 11.

                    TROOPER 1
          This is Unit 11. We are at Summit. We have
          completed assigned tour on Grid 20 to 55 East,
          everything's quiet, no sign of anything moving—
          over.

CUT TO:

74.   EXT. LABORATORY – CAPTAIN'S CAR

Captain stands at side of car with radiophone in hand. Brad and Myers are with him.

                    CAPTAIN
          Good. Hold your position. Unit 4 will meet you
          there to complete coverage of that section—over.

                    TROOPER 1
               (Filter)
          Roger, Unit 11—out.

                    CAPTAIN
               (To Brad)
          Well, that's the last Unit to check in,
          no sign of anything yet.

                    BRAD
          You've instructed them about being as quiet
          as possible, haven't you?

                    CAPTAIN
          Yes sir, and they've gone to whatever farmhouses
          and cabins they could get to, and told them not to
          make any noise!

                    BRAD
          They haven't told these people why?

                    CAPTAIN
          No sir, that is not the real reason. I've had
          them say to stay in their houses and be quiet
          because there's a killer mountain lion roaming
          the hills. I don't know if it'll do much good.

                    MYERS
          It's better than creating a state of hysteria if
          they know the truth!

                    BRAD
          Wish we had that generator. I'd like to see
          what it would do…if it worked we'd at least
          know if we're on the right track about our demon.

Radio *CRACKLES* on.

VOICE
(Filtered)
This is Trooper Unit 4 calling Captain Walker at HQ operation Firefly.
(Captain takes the mike)

CAPTAIN
This is Captain Walker. Come in Unit 4.

VOICE
(Filtered)
Have completed circuit and now at Summit—in contact with Unit 11. No activity here—over.

CAPTAIN
All right, start back down the hill the way you came and proceed back to starting point – over.

VOICE
(Filtered)
Right sir, out.

CAPTAIN
(Picks up map: examines with flashlight)
To all units of Operation Firefly—To all units Operation Firefly—as soon as you have completed your tours, start back the way you came to your starting points, and start on alternate grids—over and out.
(Indicates map)
That will give us complete coverage of all accessible areas from the base of the mountain up to Crystal Springs itself.

BRAD
(To Myers)
Crystal Springs, poor Helen, what a weekend she's having here…losing Mike and everything.

MYERS
Made any arrangements for him?

BRAD
The local mortician is contacting Mike's folks in Oregon. We'll send him there.

MYERS
That's probably best.
(Brad heads for cabin)

BRAD
I'm going to call Helen at the Inn and see how she's doing. Call me if anything happens.

Myers nods and Brad goes in. The *RADIO* crackles to life.

VOICE 1
(Filter)
Unit 7 to HQ Operation Firefly.

CAPTAIN
Come in, Unit 7, this is Headquarters Firefly.

VOICE 1
We are at first checkpoint of alternate— reporting all clear.

CAPTAIN
Roger. Wait for team Unit to meet you before proceeding.

Other units now check in and the Captain issues instructions. During this, we *FULL BACK* to *MEDIUM SHOT* including road leading up. We *SEE* and *HEAR* a large truck coming up to the cabin. It's a power company truck with large generator on it. We watch it pull up to the cabin, and Jim jumps down from the driver's seat cupolas while a driver sits behind the wheel. Jim comes over to Myers and the Captain.

                    JIM
          Here she is. Just what the Doctor ordered.

                    MYERS
          Good, Brad wondered if you could get it.

                    JIM
          Well, I started for the Airbase at Jepson, but then
          I figured it might take too long to get it, so I
          stopped off at the local Power Company and they
          gave us this mobile unit. He doesn't need it inside,
          the generator's built onto the truck.
                 (Brad comes out and sees mobile unit)

                    BRAD
                 (Pleased)
          Oh, you got it, great!
                 (Goes over to truck to examine it)
          This oughta work.
                 (To the driver)
          Run it alongside the cabin. We can tie in from there.

The driver nods, starts up and runs truck to the spot Brad shows him. The driver gets down. They raise the sides of the truck and start unloading cable to string inside.

CUT TO:

75.   CAPTAIN'S CAR

A radio unit checks in.

                    VOICE
                 (Filter)
          Unit 3 to HQ Operation Firefly. Unit 3
          to Operation Firefly—Emergency—Come in!
                 (Captain grabs mike)

CAPTAIN
Headquarters Operation Firefly to Unit 3—
Report!

CUT TO:

76.   EXT. TUCSON ROAD—NIGHT

We see a trooper at car radio reporting in. It is on a high road overlooking a small farm in the background. The farmhouse is lit up, and to the back of it a small bar is ablaze lighting the sky; over the crackle of fire, we *HEAR* the *SOUND* of gunshots.

TROOPER
(Excited)
We found it, sir! It attacked old man Tucson's farm, and we've opened fire on it!

CUT TO:

77.   EXT. CAPTAIN'S CAR

CAPTAIN
You what?

In back we *HEAR* Myers calling Brad.

CAPTAIN
Did you kill it? Over.

CUT TO:

78.   EXT. TUCSON ROAD

TROOPER
No, sir, we've fired point blank at it. It's terrible, sir. He's white hot. He's killed the old man. Please send help. I don't think we can hold him!

CUT TO:

79.

> CAPTAIN
> *(Brad, Myers and Jim are
> listening to the speaker)*
> Right, try to hold out. We'll be right there—
> over.
> *(Clicks button)*
> To all Units on Operation Firefly—Attention
> all units on Operation Firefly...
> *(Looks at map)*
> Units 9 to 13 proceed at once to Location
> Tucson farm, Tucson Road. Grids 15 East and
> Charlie North—repeat Grids 15 East and
> Charlie North—Out!
> *(Turns to Brad and others)*
> Let's go, we've got him, or he's got us!

They all hop in the car and take off!

DISSOLVE:

80. EXT. TUCSON ROAD—NIGHT

The fire is raging behind the barn as we watch the trooper climb down the bank of the hill carrying a shotgun to join his fellow trooper that is closing in and firing at the demon!

CUT TO:

81. THE DEMON

He is standing with a wide-eyed confused look on his face. He is between the burning shed and the house which is backed up against a steep mountain side...He looks to one side and then to another, as if trying to find a way to escape. In the foreground, we see the body of the farmer lying on the ground, a shotgun in his hand—his body is smoking. A dog is in a penned-up yard, in front of where the demon is trapped. He is barking and running back and forth. The monster looks at it. Its hands reach up and cover its ears. It walks toward the dog. As it weaves, it turns from multicolored to white hot.

CUT TO:

82.   DOG

Yapping and barking—is slowly covered with a beam of color, falls over and into a smoking mass of fur!

83.   EXT. ROAD

A trooper car pulls up and two troopers jump out and look at the flaming holocaust in grim amazement, and then start down the bank to join the other two troopers.

84.   SIDE OF BANK

The four troopers together are firing at the demon.

> TROOPER 1
> Look at that thing.

> TROOPER 2
> I see it, but I don't believe it!

> TROOPER 3
> What is it?

> TROOPER 4
> I don't know, but we better get it! C'mon Bill, let's get around on this side. We can keep it holed in, and catch it in crossfire.

Two troopers get up and run to the side along the base of the mountain, to the back of the burning shed…They open fire from there. The bullets hit the demon but nothing happens. It just turns toward them and looks, then looks back at the other troopers.

CUT TO:

85. EXT. ROAD

Three trooper cars pull into the band and the troopers get out to join the fight. A fire truck pulls up and the hose is unraveled and made ready.

CUT TO:

86.   AT BANK OF ROAD

Two of them take off and go to the high side of the road that looks down at the back of the house. Now the demon is hemmed in on three sides by the troopers and backed against the wall of the mountain!

CUT TO:

87.   DEMON

Looks in the direction of the new attackers on the road side, and reacts to the shooting like a cornered animal! Snarling and flailing its arms in defiance.

CUT TO:

88.   TWO TROOPERS ON BANK OF ROAD

They are standing precariously on the bank shooting down at it. One standing lower than the other…The trooper on top calls down to the one below.

                    TROOPER A
            Watch your fire, Jack! We got two boys on the
            other side of the shed!
                    (Trooper B looks back instinctively
                    and yells)

                    TROOPER B
        Right!
                    (As he turns forward again, he
                    loses his balance, and slides down
                    the hill, screaming as he goes)

                    TROOPER A
            Hold your fire! Hold your fire!
                    (They do and he starts down the hill
                    for his fallen buddy who lies there
                    with a broken leg)

CUT TO:

89.   DEMON

Looks to bank of hill where the trooper fell, and where his buddy is descending. He turns and starts for them!

CUT TO:

90.   TWO TROOPERS

The one lies there holding his leg as the other descends the bank and gets to him. As he does, he pulls at the injured trooper and looks up. The demon is approaching. They register fear at the sight in front of them. He tries to get his buddy to his feet.

                 INJURED TROOPER B
            C'mon, leave me! Get outta here!

                    TROOPER A
            No! Grab my arm!

91.   TROOPERS IN FRONT OF HOUSE

                    TROOPERS
            It's going after 'em...open fire. Maybe we

can distract it. Be careful!

They run down the bank firing as they go, trying to turn the demon toward them.

CUT TO:

92.   DEMON
Turns at this firing, and then turns back to the fallen trooper and his friend who is trying to crawl up the steep bank, but can't make it! Steadily he plods toward them.

CUT TO:

93.   TWO-SHOT TROOPERS – DEMON'S POV

They are trapped! They stand backs against the wall, their eyes widen as the Fiery Creature comes closer. One picks up his gun and fires point-blank! Shot after shot! As he does, so the ominous multicolored shroud of death covers them and they scream as they start to smoke, straighten and fall back against the bank and slowly sink to the ground—dead!

CUT TO:

94.   TWO TROOPERS (WHO CAME IN CLOSE)

Reaction to the above. The two troopers turn and run back to the hill they came from.

CUT TO:

95.   EXT. ROAD

The captain's car pulls up and Brad, Jim, and Myers with the Captain get out and look down at the fiery hell below them. The Captain talks to the Fire Warden.

CAPTAIN
Any danger that fire spreading?

FIRE WARDEN
No. Ground's still wet from the storm!

CAPTAIN
Good, then you better stay here, but be ready just in case. Don't want my men trapped.

FIRE WARDEN
Yes, sir.
(Group descends to where the Four troopers are. Trooper 1 turns to Captain and points)

TROOPER
It's in back of the house, sir.
(They look and see it)

BRAD
(Stunned)
It's unbelievable!
(Myers watches it with a strange look of fascination, like an arsonist at a fire)

MYERS
It's real. It really exists! A being from another planet!
(Brad looks over at Myers and notices the strange look on Myer's face…it bothers him)

TROOPER
(To Captain)
It killed Edwards and Martin, sir. Burned 'em to death! We've all been firing right at it, but it doesn't do any good. What should we do?

CAPTAIN
It beats me. What do you think, Curtis? What can we do?

BRAD
(Helpless)
I don't know. If bullets won't kill it…what will?

TROOPER
Maybe fire? We could set it afire with gasoline!
(Points)
Our shooting can't hurt it, but it seems to keep it hemmed in back there. If we can hold him there long enough we could get on the hill above him, pour gasoline down on him, and set him afire! And the fire unit's here, case it gets outta hand!

CAPTAIN
(To Brad)
What do you think, sir?

BRAD
It's worth trying…Think so, Ira?
(Myers is staring straight ahead at the creature, completely absorbed)

BRAD
What do you think, Ira?

MYERS
(Absently)
What?

BRAD
Should we set it on fire with gasoline?

MYERS
(Turns sharply)
Set it on fire?
(His attitude is one of disbelief)
What are you saying?

BRAD
It has to be destroyed, Ira. There's no way to control it!
(Myers stands erect, and a wild look comes to his eyes)

MYERS
Destroy it! You want to destroy the most wonderful thing that has happened to science since the beginning of time!

CAPTAIN
I've got two dead troopers down there who don't think it's so wonderful.

BRAD
(Reasoning)
The Captain's right, Ira. This isn't anything to fool with.
(Myers looks at Brad as though he were a stranger)

MYERS
Brad, YOU! You're a scientist! How can you talk like that! You want to destroy the one link we have with the Universe! The one chance we may ever have to discover the very secret of life itself?
(Brad sees Myers working into hysteria)

BRAD
Ira...I know what it means, I know what studying

it can do, for science, but this isn't a specimen we can take into a lab and dissect…This is a living Hell Fire that is capable of destroying anything it comes in contact with! It killed Mike and these troopers, and the others, and no one else should be sacrificed in the name of science or anything else!

MYERS
(Almost pleading)
But Brad, you helped to bring it into existence! You have a responsibility to…

BRAD
(Interrupts)
Yes, I have a responsibility because I did help bring it here! It's got to be stopped! Don't you understand, Ira!

MYERS
Yes! I understand! We made an agreement, we were going to reason with this being, communicated with it, show that we don't want to harm it, that we want to be friends…

BRAD
I know but…

MYERS
But because it killed in defense of itself, because it killed people that were harming it!
(Points to Captain)
You! What right did your men have to shoot at it! It had every right to kill them, that's what they were trying to do to it! Only they couldn't, and now for the sake of a few people who are already dead, you want to throw away our one chance to learn what the entire Universe is… something that might advance us a thousand

years… Why now? Why does it have to be destroyed at this moment? Why now?

BRAD

Because we have it cornered. If it gets away, we may never get the chance again… until after it has "innocently" killed more people… Don't you see, Ira…

MYERS

Yes, I see, just earlier tonight we said how sorry we felt for it, and now…

BRAD

I still feel sorry for it, Ira. I feel sorry for a rattlesnake, but I'm not going to try to reason with it!

MYERS

Well, that's where we differ…
(Myers gets up and starts to walk down the hill toward the demon)

BRAD

Ira! Come back!

MYERS

Let go of me!

BRAD

Don't be a fool, Ira! It'll kill you!

MYERS

No, it won't. It will not harm me, because I will not harm it. I won't make any noise to frighten it. I won't give it any reason to hurt me. I will think friendship and transmit that feeling to it. It is an intelligent being. It must

understand. More than you do, Brad. Now leave me alone!
> (He tears himself out of Brad's grasp and turns facing the demon. Brad hesitates a moment, then goes back to where the Captain and the group are)

CAPTAIN
Well, you tried…He's a fool!

BRAD
(Watching Myers)
Yes he is. Most brave men are!

The Captain watches Myers for a moment, then turns to the trooper next to him.

CAPTAIN
Get up on the hill with that gasoline. Just in case. Hurry! And tell the fire unit—what we intend doing…

Two of the troopers take off. Then the Captain stands up and calls.

CAPTAIN
Hold your fire…Don't make any noise of any kind. Don't shoot till I say so!
(Firing at far end ceases)

96. SHOT OF FIREMEN

They have hoses strung down the hill. Myers walks toward the house with measured steps.

97. MYERS CLOSE-UP

As he walks his eyes shine with warmth, you can see him mentally extending his hand in friendship, as he walks closer and closer to the open space between the shed that is now turned to embers, and the house.

CUT TO:

98.   GROUP SHOT

As they watch intensely.

CUT TO:

99.   MEYERS

Talking evenly, slowly…he walks through the narrow space, gets close to the rear of the house and stops for a moment; he drops his head as though in meditation.

CUT TO:

100.   BRAD CLOSE-UP

Tense.

CUT TO:

101.   CAPTAIN AND GROUP

Quietly watching.

CUT TO:

102.   TWO TROOPERS

They are climbing the hill above the demon lugging five-gallon cans of gasoline.

CUT BACK TO:

103.   MYERS CLOSE-UP

He raises his bowed head, squares his shoulders, a resolute look on his face and he walks forward into sight of the demon. Now his eyes widen as he stands but twenty-five feet away from it.

CUT TO:

104.   DEMON

It turns, sees Myers standing there. A snarl wrinkles its steaming, multi-hued face, as it sees one of its tormentors standing there seemingly unafraid.

For a moment they hold his tableau, staring at each other like an animal and its trainer...slowly Myers extends his arms and talks softly.

>   MYERS
> Friend...I am your friend...I won't harm you
>   (*smiles*).
> Friend...do you understand?

The Demon stares...a perplexed look on its face...as though it were trying to fathom what this strange being was doing.

>   MYERS
> You can feel what I am saying...can't
> you? Welcome, friend. I want to help
> you in this strange world you've stumbled
> into.
>   (*The Demon registers an intelligent
>   look, its face still confused, relaxes a
>   little...as it does the steaming colors
>   fade-in tone slightly.*)

105.   MYERS

Is encouraged by this slight display of trust by the demon...slowly now, he walks a few steps closer.

106.   DEMON

Its colors pulsate brighter as it soundlessly snarls at the advancing Myers.

> MYERS
> *(Softly, soothingly)*
> No, don't be afraid...I can't hurt you...
> I wouldn't...I'm your friend.

The demon relaxes again and the pulsating color subsides again. Myers advances still closer, arms outstretched.

> MYERS
> *(As though to a child)*
> Friend...Friend...That's right!

The demon now extends its arms slowly...mimicking Myers' gesture. Slowly he walks closer to Myers.

> MYERS
> *(Totally encouraged)*
> Yes!...Yes! You *do* understand! I knew
> you did.

He walks forward and is now within six feet of the demon. Myers looks up into the shining eyes of the creature...with a smile of trust. He is like a Missionary facing a strange headhunter! For a few moments, they stand like that, facing each other, trying to fathom each other's thoughts. When suddenly without warning the demon becomes white hot! Moves forward...slowly!

CUT TO:

107. MYERS CLOSE-UP – POV DEMON

His eyes widen at this action...and his smile fades as his eyes widen incomprehendingly. He pleads softly.

> MYERS
> No...No...I am your friend. Please don't...

As he speaks softly, now pathetically, we see the ominous multicolored pattern creep over him. He continues speaking even as his very soul is being cremated within him!

> I'm your friend...Please don't...

His clothes start to smoke.

> Please...I a-aam...

And softly, as he speaks, he stiffens, and, caught in the middle of a word...dies...

108. GROUP SHOT

They watch in transfixed horror!

109. BRAD CLOSE-UP

Tears well up in his eyes.

> BRAD
> *(Softly)*
> Ira...Ira...It killed him.

> CAPTAIN
> Well, now we know. Let's fight fire with fire!
> *(He straightens with determination and calls out)*

                    CAPTAIN
          All right, men…start shooting! Keep him
          hemmed in.
                    (Waves to hill)
          Okay! Drop that gasoline on that murdering ghoul!
          Fire Unit stand by!…Get him!
                    (They all opened fire on it)

CUT TO:

110.   TROOPERS WITH GASOLINE

From the hillside, directly above the demon, they splash the gas down on him.

CUT TO:

111.   THE DEMON

It reacts as the gas pours down on it, and it bursts into flames. But now, you can't see it…some of the gas has dropped on the edge of the house and the house starts to go up in flames too.

112.   TROOPERS ON HILL

They back away as a wall of flame shoots up the hillside.

CUT TO:

113.   CAPTAIN AND BRAD

                    CAPTAIN
          Can you see?

                    BRAD
          No! The fire's hiding it.

CAPTAIN
Think it's doing any good?

BRAD
I hope so!
(*They watch the fire, trying to see the demon. The flames lick at the small cabin, and it's a smoking pyre...but no sign of the demon...The Fire Warden comes over to the Captain and Brad*)

FIREMAN
If that thing lives through that, nothing can stop it!

CAPTAIN
(*Watching*)
Yeah...

FIREMAN
I think we better get the hoses in and put it out. It's getting a little outta hand. We don't want to take any chances on it spreading, then we'd have to blast it out!

CAPTAIN
(*Looks up*)
You got explosives with you?

FIREMAN
Sure, standard equipment.

CAPTAIN
Good, get it ready. We might blast him with it!

TROOPER
Captain, sir, if that thing's made of fire...Maybe the water will put him out too! Think so?

                    CAPTAIN
    Could be!
        (To Trooper)
    Get all the boys down here...We're gonna
    move in with the hoses...Keep the firemen
    covered, if it's still alive and rushes us...Shoot
    at it...
        (To Firemen)
    Your hoses are ready?

                    FIREMAN
    Yes, sir.

                    CAPTAIN
    Okay! Let's move it!

All the troopers, guns ready, assemble around the *FIREMAN*. They have three long hoses reaching down the hill. Now the Fire Warden gives orders and the three hoses are spread apart, at strategic points facing the cabin. He raises his hand to signal the man up at the truck and the pumper starts. Long streams of water start to arc toward the flashing pyre. As the stream hits it, the cabin's walls crumble. Now the fire becomes less and less and steam rises from the charred blackened ruins. Brad, Jim and the Captain peer ahead trying to see the demon...The water streams in and the fire is out...just smoke and steam rises out of the ruins.

                    CAPTAIN
    I don't see it! I think that did the trick!

                    FIREMAN
    Want a searchlight on it?

                    CAPTAIN
    No! If it's still alive, we'll see it better in the dark.
        (Waves to men)
    All right, move in!

Slowly, they creep closer, closer…and then…

Looming out of the center of the blackened mess…the demon rises…his multicolored body glowing and steaming in the night. It is untouched!

CUT TO:

114. GROUP REACTION

>   BRAD
>   *(Amazed)*
>   It's still Alive!

>   CAPTAIN
>   *(Disbelieving)*
>   It can't be!

The Captain recovers enough to call out.

>   CAPTAIN
>   Hit it with the water!

Now the hoses are concentrated on the demon. *CLOUDS OF STEAM* go up, but it stands there without any effect!

115. THE DEMON

Gestures wildly and starts to move forward to the group.

>   FIRE WARDEN
>   Keep those hoses on him!
>   *(The sprays keep forcing it back, as it*
>   *tries to move forward)*

116. TWO-SHOT – CAPTAIN AND FIRE WARDEN

>   WARDEN
>   We can't keep this up forever, Captain!

What should we do?

                    CAPTAIN
What d'ya mean?

                    FIRE WARDEN
                 (Points to truck)
Tankers almost empty! Got about two minutes.

                    CAPTAIN
Oh no!
              (Decides)
We'll use the explosives. Hill! Marty! Go with the Chief and set a detonation…Better go up the hill and drop the charge down in back of him. We'll try to hold him till you're set…Hurry!!!

117.   FIRE WARDEN AND THE TWO TROOPERS

Run up to the back of the truck.

CUT TO:

118.   DETONATOR TEAM

…at truck they grab loads of *EXPLOSIVES* and coils of wire and a pusher-type blast box. They load up and run along the road to the hill behind the demon.

CUT TO:

119.   BRAD

…with one hose man.

                    BRAD
How's it holding up?
            (Fireman shrugs)

CUT TO:

120. DEMON

Spray is still holding it back. It snarls and waves its arms.

CUT TO:

121. DETONATORS ON HILL

They work feverishly. They have the dynamite and caps required to wire it now and carefully lower it…like fisherman with a line.

CUT TO:

122. INSERT OF DYNAMITE

It's being lowered. It goes a ways and then snags on a small bush sticking out.

CUT TO:

123. DETONATORS

They're sweating with anxiety.

>   TROOPER 1
> It's stuck!

The Fire Warden gets down prone, looks over the side. Now gently he tugs at it.

CUT TO:

124. INSERT DYNAMITE

It's being tugged but holds…tugged again, and then it's free!

125. DETONATORS ON HILL

>   FIRE WARDEN
>   *(Exhales)*
>   It's free…don't get it too low now, we don't
>   want it getting wet!
>   *(They lower it some more)*

CUT TO:

126. CAPTAIN, BRAD, AND HOSES

They are spraying, and now the hose starts to spurt and choke as the water starts to give out. The Captain looks in desperation to the hill.

CUT TO:

127. DETONATORS

They are giving one last twist to the wires attached to the plunger and they're finished! They raise their hands to signal the Captain below.

CUT TO:

128. CAPTAIN AND HOSE CREW

One hose is dead and the other two are sputtering. The Captain looks to the hill…sees the raised arms.

CUT TO:

>   CAPTAIN
>   *(Calls)*
>   Good! They're all set…all right. Fire your guns at
>   it and run for cover. The blast is set!

129. GROUP SHOT

They drop everything, make it back to the far slope facing the demon, firing as they run.

The Captain calls out.

> CAPTAIN
> Let her go!!!

CUT TO:

130.   DETONATORS ON HILL

The Fire Warden stands hands on plunger.

> WARDEN
> Let's hope that charge didn't get wet!
> *(Takes a deep breath, and pushes down)*

CUT TO:

131.   LONG SHOT – CABIN AND DEMON

A tremendous blast rocks the area, blowing charred debris into the air. The *SOUND* echoes and re-echoes in the hollow!

CUT TO:

132.   GROUP SHOT

Lying prone, they cover their heads with their arms for protection.

133.   LONG SHOT OF BLAST AREA

Thick smoke covers the ground and rises into the air.

134.   GROUP

Brad and Captain look but can't see through the dense smoke.

CAPTAIN
Do you see it?

BRAD
No! Smoke too thick.

FIREMAN
It'll clear up in a minute.

CAPTAIN
(Calls)
Keep your guns ready!

Now silently they watch and wait…The smoke clears…and they look…nothing…

CAPTAIN
(Whispers)
See anything?

BRAD
No.

They wait and watch…nothing stirs. They wait some more. It's quiet. The Captain takes his gun out.

CAPTAIN
Let's make sure!
(Fires his pistol five times, nothing moves)
What d'ya think?

BRAD
I don't see anything moving!

CAPTAIN
(Stands up, happily)
Okay. Looks like that got it!
(Jim walks over)

> JIM
> Guess that did it, sir...Nothing could live through that!

> BRAD
> *(Smiles)*
> Sure looks like it...

Now one by one they stand up, and a feeling of relief goes through the group.

> CAPTAIN
> All right, let's go down, boys, and take a look...
> *(To troopers)*
> Mason...Clay, go up to the road and shine some spots down at the cabin...
> *(The troopers salute and take off)*

> CAPTAIN
> *(To Brad)*
> Let's go.

They descend the hill, and head for the site. The blast has torn away part of the hill below, crested a landslide, and covered part of the cabin and the area behind it where Myers was killed.

The searchlights go on now...we can see the area clearly...Brad, and the Captain and the others poke around in the debris...but find nothing.

> CAPTAIN
> Well, I guess that does it! Don't see no sign of our flaming friend.

> TROOPER
> Guess that blast kinda blew out his flames, huh, Cap'n?

                    CAPTAIN
                  (Relieved)
              Yeah…Sure did!

They all laugh sort of nervously, but with relief!

135.   TWO-SHOT OF FIREMEN

                    FIREMAN 1
        Well, Billy, for your first week on mountain
        patrol, you can now say you've put out the
        worst kinda fire you'll ever see!

                  FIREMAN BILLY
                (Young blond kid)
        Yeah…After this I guess a forest fire's gonna
        seem like a weenie roast!
                  (They laugh)

CUT TO:

136.   JIM AND BRAD
Brad's looking at the landslide of earth.

                      JIM
                (Sees him looking)
        Think the monster's buried under there?

                      BRAD
        I don't know.
                    (Sighs)
        Poor Ira…What a way to go…

                      JIM
        Yeah…
              (Captain comes into scene)

CAPTAIN
Well, that does it, Dr. Curtis.
(Looks down)
Sure tough about Dr. Myers…he was a close friend of yours, wasn't he?

BRAD
I asked him to come up here.

CAPTAIN
Now, don't go blaming yourself. It wasn't your fault. He just guessed wrong all the way around.

BRAD
(Looks up)
How's that?

CAPTAIN
Well, he thought it could be reasoned with, and thought it couldn't be destroyed…he was wrong both times!

BRAD
Yes…

CAPTAIN
Well, I gotta get this show on the road…Chief… You and your fire-crew can take off soon as you're all cleaned up…

CHIEF
Right…Let's go, boys.

Firemen start taking equipment.

CAPTAIN
All right, boys, back to your assigned units and regular duties. Unit 9 will stay here

tonight. And keep the road closed. No one gets in. We'll get the casualties out in the morning.

137.   CLOSE-UP—BRAD

Stands thinking. Jim pats him on the shoulder.

                    JIM
C'mon, Brad, snap out of it. It's all over.
                (Brad smiles)

                    BRAD
I hope so.

                    JIM
Sure it is! Look, can you get me a room at the Inn tonight? I'm too bushed to travel back to town.

                    BRAD
Yeah, I think so.

                    JIM
Good, I'll buy you dinner to celebrate.

                    BRAD
You'll have to buy two. My financee's up there.

                    JIM
                (smiles)
I'm game. I'm on an expense account.

Captain comes in.

                    CAPTAIN
If you boys are ready to go, I'll run you back to the hotel.

                        JIM
　Sure are.

                        BRAD
              (Hesitates)
　Captain, you're leaving some men here tonight,
　aren't you?

                        CAPTAIN
　Yes.
              (Laughs)
　Why? You think that thing's still alive after all
　we put it through?

                        BRAD
　I guess not, but it might be wise not to take any
　chances.

                        CAPTAIN
　Well, he would've reared his ugly head by now if
　he was, but...My boys will be in radio contact
　and if anything does develop, they could get help
　immediately. But, believe me, that thing's been
　blasted right out of this world, or I miss my guess.

                        BRAD
　Yeah! C'mon, I'll take you up on that dinner, Jim.

They walk toward the road and we...

DISSOLVE:

138.　INT. INN – DINING ROOM

We *FADE-IN* on a *BIG HEAD CLOSE-UP* of a fat face. The mouth's wide open and a loud yell comes out of it. The *CAMERA PULLS BACK* to reveal a jolly fat man in cowboy regalia, giving a loud *WHOOP!* He stands in front of a microphone on the bandstand, surrounded by a typical cowboy band. They play the last eight bars of a song. Everyone applauds and they swing into a soft ballad. As our *CAMERA MOVES THROUGH* the crowded dance floor to a table at the far end of the room, Brad, Helen, Jim, and the flaxen-haired shock victim, Betty Ann, sit quietly watching the dancers. They are all starting to eat, all except Betty Ann, who sits quietly with her head down. Helen sees this, gets up, and goes around to Betty Ann. Tenderly, she puts her arm around her.

                        HELEN
You all right, Betty Ann?

                     BETTY ANN
                   (Smiles wanly)
Yes…

                        HELEN
Maybe you should've rested more.

                     BETTY ANN
No, I wanted to come down. I couldn't stand being up there alone. S'funny…

                        HELEN
What?

                     BETTY ANN
All that's happened, and yet, they're laughing and dancing.

                         JIM
                   (leans over)
There was no sense telling them. It would only have started a panic and now that it's over, they need not ever know. Right?

                   BETTY ANN
I guess so, just doesn't seem fair. My Willis

being gone.
(Starts to cry)
...and no one knows.

HELEN
(Comforting)
We know, Betty Ann. After all, we're kind of in the same boat with you. We lost two close friends.

Betty looks up quickly.

BETTY ANN
Oh, I'm sorry. I've been so lost in my own misery, I almost forgot, please forgive me bein' so selfish and thinking about myself.

HELEN
(Smiles softly)
I think Willis would've wanted you to keep your chin up, wouldn't he have?

BETTY ANN
(Smiles; cries tears)
Yes, he would. You shoulda known Will. He was so wonderful! He...

HELEN
C'mon now, that's enough talk, better start eating. Mr. Hunter's ordered a big dinner for us and we don't want to waste it, do we?

JIM
(Joking)
You better not. The Government's buying and you know how they hate to waste money!

They all laugh except Brad, who's thinking.

                        JIM
        Right, Brad?

                        BRAD
        What?

                        JIM
        Hey, we gonna have trouble with you too?
        C'mon, dig in.

                        BRAD
        Oh, sorry. I was just thinking.

Helen goes back to her chair…looks closely at Brad.

                        HELEN
        What about?

                        BRAD
                    (Dismissing it)
        Oh, you know…

                        HELEN
        Brad. Everything's all right now, isn't it? I mean,
        it's all over. There isn't any chance of…

                        BRAD
                    (Lightening)
        Naaw…of course not, I…

He leans over and kisses her lightly.

                        BRAD
                    (Continues)
        You're just marrying a worry wart, didn't you
        know?

CUT TO:

139.   FULL SHOT OF ROOM

The song ends, the people applaud, and the loudspeaker announces a dance break. Everyone goes to their tables.

The *CAMERA PANS* to the entrance to the room, and we discover the Sheriff standing in the door, hat in hand, scanning the room. He spots Brad's table and walks over.

> SHERIFF
> Good evenin', folks.

> BRAD
> *(Apprehensive)*
> Anything wrong, Sheriff?

> SHERIFF
> *(Smiles)*
> Should there be? Naaw, I just come in to see how the little lady was makin' out.

> BETTY ANN
> Just fine, thank you kindly.

> SHERIFF
> That's good. I, uh, also wanted to apologize for not believin' ya, Doc. 'Fraid it was all a little over a small town cop's head.

> BRAD
> You weren't alone, Sheriff.

> SHERIFF
> But anyway, I'm glad it's all finished and come out all right.

                        BRAD
                    (Reflective)
                  Yeah, all finished.
                   (Changes subject)
              Uh, join us for a little drink?

                       SHERIFF
         No thanks, I'm on duty. I'm sorta the official
         bouncer here during these Saturday night
         dances. Well, didn't mean to interrupt yer dinner.
         I better get out front. See ya!

He leaves.

                        HELEN
                You know, people are nice.

                        BRAD
                    (Takes her hand)
                 Only to nice people.

Brad and Helen look warmly at each other.

                         JIM
                Hey! Break it up, let's eat!

They start eating the appetizers and the *CAMERA MOVES INTO CLOSE-UP* of fork being dipped into cocktail glass, as we...

CROSSFADE:

140.   INT. TROOPER'S CAR ON TUCSON ROAD – SAME
       NIGHT

Parked on the road above the burning incident. We *CROSSFADE* into a *CLOSE-UP* of fork being dipped into a can of hash that one of the trooper's is eating. Between them, they have a thermos of coffee and crackers, etc. Trooper behind wheel hands crackers to his buddy.

> TROOPER 1
> *(Mock graciousness)*
> Now this is the way to spend Saturday night.
> A nice, quiet dinner for two, soft lights, and…

> TROOPER 2
> Aaaa, shaddup! Saturday night and we have
> to play babysitter to an ex-monster! As if we
> didn't do enough helping catch that thing, we
> have to draw graveyard detail!

> TROOPER 1
> Well, I think we should be grateful we're here,
> it coulda been the other way around!

> TROOPER 2
> What'd ya mean?

> TROOPER 1
> We coulda been down there, and that livin'
> ball of fire coulda been up here holdin' a wake
> for us.

> TROOPER 2
> Yeah, guess so. Sure was unbelievable,
> wasn't it?

> TROOPER 1
> I still don't believe it! But I'm glad it's over.

We start a *PAN SHOT* from the car down the hill and blend into a *CLOSE-UP* of the mound of earth down below. As the music sets an ominous key, we watch the mound start to crack and fissure at the top, as if something underneath it were moving! It moves for a moment…then stops.

CUT TO:

141. BACK TO TROOPERS IN CAR

The radio crackles.

> VOICE
> Trooper Unit 9…Trooper Unit 9.
> This is HQ…over.

Trooper 1 picks up microphone.

> TROOPER 1
> HQ…HQ…This is 9. That you, Parker? Over…

> VOICE
> Yeah, how's everything down there?

> TROOPER 1
> Situation normal. Everything's real quiet.
> No change…over.

> VOICE
> Anyone been around?

> TROOPER 1
> Few people came to see the fire. Wanted to know what the explosion was. We told 'em the Army was testing something and turned 'em back.

> VOICE
> Good, no one goes past the barricade.

> TROOPER 1
> Right. Hey, when do we get relieved?

> VOICE
> Six a.m. tomorrow morning.

> TROOPER 1
> What! Hey, ask the Captain about that!

> VOICE
> Can't. He took off for L.A. for the weekend. Goodnight! Over and out!

Trooper jams down microphone. Looks to his buddy.

> TROOPER 1
> Well, how about that!

Trooper 2 slumps down in the seat and pushes his hat down over his eyes.

> TROOPER 2
> Call me when the sun comes up!

Now from offstage, we *HEAR* the loud *HONKING* of an automobile horn! Blast after blast…and the troopers jump erect.

> TROOPER 1
> Someone's really layin' on that horn!

> TROOPER 2
> Down at the barricade, let's go.

CUT TO:

142. EXT. TROOPER'S CAR

SHOT of trooper's car lights going on, and car takes off down the road.

We *HOLD* on the spot where the car was for a moment and listen to the insistent blaring of the horn, and then start a slow *PAN* down to the mound of earth. It starts to quake slightly and then more, and more. Until now, it cracks wide open from the pressure being exerted under it, until finally, it breaks open and the giant multi-hued demon pokes through! It is still alive!

The monster pulls itself erect and stands there, listening...for the moment, everything is silent and then the car HORN starts blasting away again. The demon grabs at its ears in pain, weaves, and writhes looking first one way and then another. Now it weaves down off the mound and then takes off toward the backside of the flat land, walking, and then half-running as it clutches its head in its hands, until it is lost around the far side of the hill!

CUT TO:

143.   EXT. BARRICADE—NIGHT

The police car has just pulled up to this side of a barricade thrown across the road. The troopers get out and walk past it to an open convertible with four teenagers in it. They're a happy group, dressed for dancing.

                    TROOPER 1
             All right, what is it, a wedding?

                       BOY 1
              What d'ya mean, officer?

                    TROOPER 1
              What's all the noise about?

                       BOY 1
              Well, we want to get through.

                    TROOPER 1
                    (Points to sign)
              Ya go to school, don't ya? Can't ya read?
              Road closed.

Boy in back of car pipes up.

> BOY 2
> It don't say positively!

All the kids think that's funny, and laugh.

144. CLOSE-UP TROOPER 2

Trying to keep a straight face.

> TROOPER 1
> Well, I'm saying it now. Positively!

> TROOPER 2
> What do you kids want up here so late, anyway? There's nothing around for miles.

> BOY 1
> Isn't this the road to Crystal Springs Inn?

> TROOPER 2
> No. You missed that road about a mile back.

> GIRL
> I told ya, Raymond, this wasn't the right way!

> TROOPER 2
> *(Points)*
> Look, turn around and go back to the fork, and take the left there. It's about two miles from there.
> *(Smiles at kid)*
> Goin' dancing, huh?

> GIRL 1
> Gotta meet my folks—if we ever get there.

> BOY 1
> All right, all right! Get off my back will ya? I'll get us there.

(*To Trooper 2*:)
Thanks for the directions, Friday.

Expertly wheels the car around and the kids wave back.

TROOPER 1
(Calls)
And lay off that horn!

BOY 1
(Smiling)
Ya mean like this?

And he lays on the horn but good as he guns the car away. The horn blaring loudly, the kids laugh.

CUT TO:

145.   TWO-SHOT

The troopers stand hands on hips watching.

TROOPER 1
Fresh kids! Like to run 'em in.

TROOPER 2
(Laughing)
You were a kid yourself once, weren't you?

TROOPER 1
No, I wasn't! I started out life as a mean old man.

He laughs and his buddy joins him.

TROOPER 2
C'mon, Scrooge, let's get back up that lonesome road…

They walk back to their car as we...

DISSOLVE

146.   EXT. FORK OF ROAD—NIGHT

The kids' car pulls up to a dusty stop, and they look at marker.

>   BOY 1
> What's it say?

>   BOY 2
> This is it...
>   *(Points)*
> That way.

>   BOY 1
>   *(Honks horn)*
> Roger Wilco!

>   GIRL
> Do you have to keep blasting that thing?

>   BOY 2
> Sure! It helps my frustrations. You don't want
> me to grow up to be an *ADULT* delinquent, do ya?
>   *(He laughs and honks the horn continuously*
>   *as he wheels the car up the new road)*

CUT TO:

147.   EXT. WOODS ALONGSIDE ROAD

In the dense foliage we see the glowing light of the demon as it makes its way through the underbrush...we watch it come up the bank, onto the road, from the distance we *HEAR* the *SOUND* of the *HORN* honking and the creature covers its ears, picks up in the direction the sound comes from, goes over the road and down into the brush...It is following the sound, but going in a straight line to it cross country!

148.   EXT. CRYSTAL SPRING INN—NIGHT

The kids pull up in front of the Inn. A long rustic lodge affair with a veranda running the length of it…Over the front is a paper bearing the legend: "Saturday Night Dance…Come as you are." Several cars are parked in front. Raymond honks the horn loudly as he pulls up. *SHERIFF KEMMER* comes down the front steps annoyed, and walks to the car.

                    SHERIFF
          Hey! Hey! Stop that racket! You'll wake the dead!

                    BOY 1
          That'd be a good trick! You gonna park it, boy?

                    SHERIFF
          I ain't no boy! I'm the Sheriff!

                    BOY 1
                (Shrinks)
          Oh, sorry, sir…uh…where do I park it?

                    SHERIFF
          Parkin' lot's full up…
                (Points)
          Leave it out front here, somewhere.

                    BOY 1
          Yes sir.

Guns it and parks it to the side.

CUT TO:

149.   EXT. INN DINING ROOM

Group at table have just finished eating dinner, and are on dessert. They watch the couples on the floor dancing...Jim finishes and exhales loudly, patting his middle contentedly.

                    JIM
Whew! That was good...weren't it, Betty Ann?

                BETTY ANN
Real good...Thank you!

                    JIM
Brad, care for a short one for after dinner?

                  BRAD
No, thanks...I've had it!

CAMERA PULLS BACK for *MEDIUM SHOT* into the table next to our principals; seated at it are two middle-aged couples, laughing and drinking. Our four teenagers come into the scene, and go over to the table.

                  GIRL 2
Surprise!

She leans over and kisses one of the women, and then kisses the bald-headed man next to her right, on the pate, hugging him from behind.

                  GIRL 2
Hi, Daddy!

The people at the table look up pleasantly shocked.

CUT TO:

150.   CLOSE-UP GROUP

                  DADDY
Marcie! What are you doing here? I thought you were staying home.

                        GIRL 2
            We decided to take a ride and help you old
            folks celebrate.
                    (Turns to other kids)
            Ready?

They are, together they sing Happy Anniversary to Mr. and Mrs. Kramer…and then applaud themselves loudly…Marcie produces a small gift and gives it to mother.

                        MOTHER
                    (Looks surprised)
            For me?

                        MARCIE
            …and Daddy! Hope you like it!

While she opens the gift, the other kids go over and ad lib congratulations. Mother opens the gift. It's a small compact.

                        MOTHER
            Oh, a compact. It's beautiful.

Looks up and puckers a kiss at Marcie…She hands it to Daddy.

                        DADDY
            Beautiful! Just what I always wanted…
                    (Everyone laughs)

                        MARCIE
                    (Pouts)
            Oh, daddy, I wanted to get you something too,
            but I didn't have enough money.

                        DADDY
            Well, I'll just have to increase your allowance
            next year!

CUT TO:

151. BRAD'S TABLE

They all watch the scene at the next table. Helen looks at Brad warmly.

> HELEN
> Maybe some day our children will surprise us, huh?

> BRAD
> I hope so.

> JIM
> *(To Betty Ann)*
> Care to dance awhile?

> BETTY ANN
> I would really like to, but I don't think I should... Outta respect.

> JIM
> You're right...I'm sorry, I forgot.

Music ends and people go back to their tables.

> JIM
> Too late, set's over anyway...

CUT TO:

152. BANDSTAND

The heavyset man makes an announcement.

> FAT MAN
> All right, folks, take a few minutes breather and get ready for some real dancin'...cause in a few

minutes we'll have a real ol' fashioned square dance.

Everyone applauds and yippees.

CUT BACK TO:

153.   BRAD'S TABLE

>   JIM
> A square dance! That's all I need after a nine-course dinner.
>   *(To Betty Ann)*
> Want to get some air?

>   BETTY ANN
> Don't mind if I do…kinda stuffy in here.

>   JIM
>   *(To Brad and Helen)*
> Care to join us?

Brad looks at Helen, she nods.

>   BRAD
> Yeah, good idea.

They get up and start across the floor to the front entrance.

CUT TO:

154.   EXT. FRONT VERANDA

They come out and the boys light cigarettes. The Sheriff is standing there.

>   SHERIFF
> Takin' a breather?

BRAD
(Down)
Yeah.

SHERIFF
You look tuckered out, Doc.

Helen walks over and locks her arm around Brad.

HELEN
(Lightly)
I think the day's excitement is catching up to my strong silent man…
(Leans up and kisses him)
Huh?

BRAD
(Still down)
Yeah, I guess so…

Helen takes him by the arm and leads him to a quiet corner.

HELEN
Come here.
(Stands him there and looks squarely at him)
Brad…what's wrong?

BRAD
Nothing, why?

HELEN
I know something's been bothering you all night. Tell me…No fair keeping secrets from your bride-to-be.

BRAD
It's nothing…really.

HELEN
Is it Mike and Dr. Myers?

BRAD
I don't know. I just got a funny feeling.

HELEN
It's that monster, isn't it?
(Brad nods silently)

HELEN
(Sighs)
I thought so. You think it's still alive, don't you?
(Brad nods slowly again)

HELEN
Then why don't you do something about it?
Why didn't you say anything?

BRAD
I don't know. Maybe because I wanted to believe it's dead. Don't you see, Helen, if it isn't dead, after all the punishment we put it through, nothing could destroy it!

HELEN
So you buried your head in the sand, hoping it'll go away, like a bad dream, huh?

BRAD
I guess so…but everyone else says it's dead, it hasn't shown up. The area's guarded. It must be!

HELEN
Except you don't think so.

BRAD
That's just it…It's not anything I think…

it's something I feel! I can feel it…like a
hot blast furnace breathing down my neck!

HELEN

I think you're just exhausted…You should be…
You better get some rest. You'll feel better in
the morning.

BRAD
(Smiles)
All right, nurse.

HELEN

Think I'll turn in too…Oh, darn!

BRAD

What's the matter?

HELEN

Left my purse in the dining room.

BRAD

I'll get it for you.

HELEN

No, you stay here and relax…You've done
enough running for one day.
(Over her shoulder)
Just be a minute.

She goes in door as we

CUT TO:

155.   INT. DINING ROOM

Helen crosses the deserted dance floor toward the table. As she does, the fat man on the bandstand is up at the microphone.

156. CLOSE-UP FAT MAN

He blows into the mike testing it.

                FAT MAN
        All right, folks…get ready for the square
        dance! Get ready to…Folks! Can ya
        hear me?

The *SOUND* is out on the speakers. He taps mike.

                FAT MAN
        Durn thing's out.

He turns to guitar man who has speaker control next to him.

                FAT MAN
        Roy? Turn that volume up, will ya…this
        thing's out.

157. CLOSE-UP GUITAR MAN

He leans over and twirls a control knob…and the volume comes on real loud in a loud squealing sound from feedback.

CUT TO:

158. HELEN AT TABLE

She's looking for her purse. She can't find it. She looks to a serving table that is up against the wall by the full-length French doors near where their table is placed. As she does, we *HEAR* the microphone loud, piercing, feedback *SOUND* from offstage. She goes to the serving table and looks around for her purse. She finds it and is about to turn, when her attention is drawn to the French windows…What she sees there makes her eyes widen in horror! For outside, weaving and writhing in pain and holding its head, is the demon from Dimension X!

She stands there terrified, unable to move! The squealing of the microphone feedback is driving the monster into a tortured frenzy! Twisting and turning, and as it does, it blindly falls forward right through the large glass windows and pitches headlong into the room. The sound of the glass crashing captures everyone's attention and they see this giant mess of swirling colors stagger blindly into the dining room, and into the dance area right past Helen…

Now everyone sees it and the place turns into pandemonium as the women start screaming and people back away…trying to escape this horrifying intruder!

159.   FRONT VERANDA

Brad and Jim *HEAR* the crash and the wild screaming and look at each other in wonderment…They turn and rush inside, the Sheriff in tow.

CUT TO:

160.   INT. ENTRANCE TO DINING ROOM

Brad and Jim stop at door, and look inside.

CUT TO:

161.   GROUP AT A TABLE CLOSE-UP

Caught before they could move, they stare in uncomprehending fear…the women screaming! We see them covered with the deadly crazy quilt of color and succumb.

The Demon turns to another couple cornered…the man and woman stand fear-stricken. We see their reactions as it gets closer and the man stands in front of her to protect her. He even raises his hand to strike at the monster when he is covered with the blanket of death and…his hand in midair.

162.   BACK TO BRAD AND JIM AT DOORWAY

They can't believe it!

BRAD
Oh God! I knew it was still alive!

JIM
What can we do?

BRAD
I don't know.

SHERIFF
(Drawing his gun)
I'll stop it!

JIM
That won't do any good. It can't be killed!

SHERIFF
It might draw its attention though.

JIM
That's too dangerous, might hit somebody.

BRAD
If we could only lure it outside away from the people.

JIM
If that microphone were portable, the noise would distract it.

Helen comes running up to them.

HELEN
Oh, Brad, Brad!
(Falls into his arms)
What can we do!

> BRAD
> Get Betty Ann and wait in the car. Hurry!

> HELEN
> I don't want to leave you!

> BRAD
> Go on! Honk the horn if you have…
> *(Gets idea)*
> The horn! That's it! Sheriff, Jim, get out front, and start honking all the car horns you can! That'll do it! That's the answer.

> JIM
> What do we do after it's out by the cars?

> BRAD
> Jim…listen carefully. We can't destroy it. Maybe we can send it BACK where it came from! I'm going on ahead and hook up the generator…at the lab! You get in your car and lure it up there with your car horn; you understand? It'll follow the noise…go slow enough so it will follow you, and lead it up to the lab…I'll have everything ready when you get there! Let's go!

They run out of the room.

CUT TO:

163. EXT. FRONT OF INN

They come out of the entrance…Brad runs to his car, with Helen and Betty Ann, whom they grabbed on the steps. He gets in the car, and starts *HONKING* the horn *LOUDLY!* Jim and the Sheriff get to other cars and *BLAST* the horns!

CUT TO:

164.   INT. DINING ROOM

The demon is about to attack a man in the corner when off stage we *HEAR THE SOUND* of the horns blasting loudly! The demon stops in its tracks and turns in the direction of the sound. It raises its hands to its ears, and weaves around and then slowly turns in the direction of the door and starts out.

CUT TO:

165.   EXT. FRONT OF INN

The demon comes to the front, and stands on the veranda thrashing its arms, its face contorted with pain!

CUT TO:

166.   BRAD IN CAR

Waves to Jim and Sheriff. Brad stops his horn, and guns the car.

CUT TO:

167.   JIM GETS IN CAR

He calls to Sheriff at the next car.

> JIM
> Stop your horn, and don't let anyone move, you go it?

Sheriff stops horn, and nods. Jim keeps *BLASTING* his horn, and looks to see what the demon is doing.

CUT TO:

168.   DEMON

It looks in the direction of Jim's car and starts for it!

CUT TO:

169.   JIM – INT. CAR

He starts the motor while he keeps the horn honking, looking over his shoulder. He sees the monster coming. The motor dies. Registering the excitement of the moment, he tries starting it again. All the while blasting the horn…it whirls…and finally catches when the monster is almost to him…now he takes off slowly, and the monster follows him…like a dog following meat on a stick…Slowly the car goes down the road away from the lodge, the horn *BLASTING*, the demon following behind it, until the car is lost to the darkness, and we see the fading illumination of the pursuing demon!

170.   INT. BRAD'S CAR

He looks intently to the road in front of him and drives slowly down the winding road.

>   BRAD
>   Let's just hope it works.

As he drives, a car coming toward him with bright lights, zooms by…honking…Brad veers the car to avoid hitting him.

>   HELEN
>   Look out!

>   BRAD
>   That was close. That's all we would've
>   needed now.

>   HELEN
>   How much further?

BRAD
Less than a mile—wonder how Jim's doing?

CUT TO:

171.   JIM'S CAR

It moves slowly, with the horn blaring, and the demon following with a half-walking, half-running gait.

172.   INT. JIM'S CAR

He holds the horn down, and looking through the rear view mirror, we see the demon in it. As he drives, we see the bright lights of the car that passed Brad earlier coming toward us. The other car *HEARING* Jim's horn, join in as it passes, and goes by the monster, without stopping.

CUT TO:

173.   INT. PASSING CAR

Horror on man and woman's faces as they see monster…and the car goes out of control and goes over the road! Horn blowing, then stops—crash of falling car.

174.   DEMON

The horns have now confused it and it stops…and turns as if to follow the other cars.

175.   INT. JIM'S CAR

He stops, and honks loudly, softly cursing the distraction…watches the monster and throws the car into reverse! He backs up close to the monster…honking wildly…and then the monster turns and starts after him again, and Jim starts up again in the slow weird procession…

CUT TO:

176. EXT. LAB NIGHT

Brad pulls up in front of the cabin and jumps out of the car, and runs inside…The driver of the power truck is there in the easy chair, he had been sleeping! He jumps up when Brad comes in.

> DRIVER
> Where ya been? I thought you forgot about me!

> BRAD
> Good grief…we did, but I'm glad you're here…
> C'mon we got work to do.

Brad goes to the equipment and starts checking.

> DRIVER
> What's been happening, anyway?

> BRAD
> Look, there's no time to explain. You'll know in
> a few minutes if everything works out. Let's
> get these generators hooked together.

The cables had been strung into the room, and lay strung across the floor. Brad picks one up and checks the plug connection. He looks at the line of sockets in the generators he has against the wall. He tries hooking them together.

> BRAD
> Oh no, the wrong size!

Helen comes to the workbench.

> HELEN
> Anything I can do?

                    BRAD
        No—YES! Get outside, keep your eye on
        the road, and let me know when they're
        coming!

Helen leaves. Brad talks as he examines equipment.

                    BRAD
                  (To driver)
        Got a four-prong jack out there?

                    DRIVER
        Nope.

                    BRAD
        Gonna have to splice them together,
        then...

Brad starts unscrewing the faceplate of his power deck.

                    BRAD
        Cut the jack off that cable and peel the
        wire, will ya?

Driver does so...watches Brad at work.

                    DRIVER
        Think your capacitors will hold this extra load?

                    BRAD
        I don't know, but it's too late to find out!

                    DRIVER
        What you trying to do anyway?

                    BRAD
                  (Smiles)
        Make lightning!

> DRIVER
> Make lightning! You might blow us all to kingdom come!

> BRAD
> *(Working)*
> Have to chance it! There!

Lifts off faceplates and takes cable from driver, as he pulls switch, yells toward door.

> BRAD
> Helen, see anything?

> HELEN
> *(Offstage)*
> Not yet!

Brad turns back to work…splicing the wires. Now offstage we HEAR the sound of a horn blasting.

> HELEN
> *(Offstage)*
> Brad, they're coming!

> BRAD
> All right!
> *(Finishes splice)*
> There, that's got it!

Now he goes to tubes, and checks them. Sets dials…picks up logbook and reads as he sets switches.

> BRAD
> *(Reading as he works)*
> 1500 a…
> *(Turns dial)*

He reads and sets some more. The *SOUND* of the horn gets louder.

CUT TO:

177. HELEN AT DOOR

> HELEN
> Brad, they're at the bottom of the road!

CUT TO:

178.

BRAD

> All right...I'm almost set!

Now he works feverishly...checking out, this level, against the logbook. That switch against the written data...He makes a quick check and goes to the door. The horn is louder as we...

CUT TO:

179. EXT. ROAD

Jim's car is just coming up the road, horn blaring. The monster following. The car pulls up to the door with the demon about a hundred and fifty yards behind. Jim blasts the horn as he gets out and calls to Brad.

CUT TO:

> JIM
> Brad! What now? How do we get him in the lab?

> BRAD
> I can't do it with the equipment. The speaker system's out. Helen, Betty Ann...come inside. Jim, you too! Stand there and scream at the top of your lungs...keep screaming.

                           JIM
            That'll be easy.

They all get in the doorway, as Jim sees the demon but a few yards away…lets go of the horn…and runs in the door. The demon gets near the car…that now is silent. He stands there flailing his arms in indecision at the now quiet car…then turns toward the door where his tormentors stand.

180.   JIM, HELEN, AND BETTY ANN IN THE DOORWAY

They all stand looking in fright…and Betty Ann emits a cry of fright that comes naturally…Now Jim and Helen join the chorus.

The monster moves toward them, grasping his ears, as their piercing shrieks drive him painfully forward!

As he walks toward them, Jim and Helen move back in the room, but Betty Ann stands rooted in the door, too petrified to move. Jim grabs her arm and pulls her bodily back into the room. They scream as they back up in the face of the advancing demon!

CUT TO:

181.   INT. LAB

Now they are inside, and the demon comes in the door.

CUT TO:

182.   BRAD AT POWER SWITCH

                           BRAD
            Keep screaming, and back toward to me, till I
            say stop…Pray that this works!

They backed toward Brad…and he throws the power switch; a large shock of light breaks through the equipment that lights the room, and puts out the lights! Now in the darkness to see the monster standing in brilliant colors as the tubes light up.

                             BRAD
               Stop screaming!

They stop and stand looking in awe as the demon, now in the room, stops in his tracks. The tubes light with color, and a spectrum of fog surrounds them and slowly spreads across the room and covers the entire far wall of the room…eddying, spiraling colors steam and float until the entire wall of the cabin is obliterated.

Now the steam solidifies and becomes a translucent membrane!!! The equipment crackles, with bright flashes of light, and the center of the membrane starts to burn open…and we can see the other world! We see weird landscapes, covered in brilliant, strange colors!…mountains, blue trees, and a vaporous fog surrounding it all…

The demon stands watching all this, and a look of what must be called exultation comes over his face…now he turns to Brad, Helen and the others, and his face turns to a scowl. He makes a half-hearted sweep at them, and then looks back to the light emanating from this world, makes a decision and goes to the opening, and starts to crawl through…

As he does so, an arm of another creature reaches out and wraps around the back of the demon and gently assists the monster through the hole!

CUT TO:

183.   BRAD AT SWITCH

Brad and Helen and the others watch in wide-eyed amazement at what they've just seen. Then Brad breaks the spell! Reaches up and *PULLS* the power switch! The crackling stops and the tear in the membrane starts to close…then it disappears and slowly the mass of swirling color disappearing. The color around the tubes fades, and the lights in the cabin gradually come on…The shock of what they have just seen leaves them all numb for a moment and then Brad speaks.

                             BRAD
               It's over!

Betty Ann starts to sob softly. Helen gets to Brad and…

FADE-OUT:

                    HELEN
    Oh Brad!

                    BRAD
    All over…for good, this time!

The driver who was standing at the corner finally gets his voice back.

                    DRIVER
    I can't believe it! Did it really happen?

                    JIM
    It sure did.

                    BRAD
    It never will again!

With that he picks up a walking stick standing in the corner, and reaches up and smashes both the tubes.

                    BRAD
    Never again!

                    DRIVER
    (Catching breath)
    Whew, what a frightening experience!

                    BRAD
    Yeah…but I wonder if we were as frightened
    as he was!!!

They look at each other reflectively as we…

DISSOLVE:

                  THE END

Lyrics

I'm Drowning My Sorrows
(Music by Eddie Brandt. Lyrics by Paul Frees)

[Released on January 20, 1957. Reached Number 24 on the charts on February 27, 1957.]

> I'm drowning my sorrows in oceans of tears
> Just cryin' my heart out but nobody hears
> I'm drowning my sorrows, it's hard to forget
> That I've ever known you, that we ever met
>
> Goodbye my love, my sweet, my own
> Farewell to all of the dreams we have known
> And so, my dear, our love story ends
> We started as lovers and parted as friends
> A million tomorrows, I'll never be free
> I'm drowning my sorrows, please come back to me

Written for Spike Jones, submitted 1951
(Courtesy of Jordan R. Young)

October 18, 1951

Mr. Spike Jones
Jefferson Davis Hotel
Montgomery, Alabama

Dear Spike:

Here are the numbers we discussed in Las Vegas and a couple of others. I had better tell you about each one individually and the music involved. As you can see, I have taken excerpts for the opera pieces and, although they may not make sense in the reading, specifically "Rigoletto" and "Barber of Seville," they do figure out correctly in meter to music as I have written it.

What I would like to do when you get back is sit down with your arranger and show him how the music fits the lyrics I have written, and he can write it accordingly. Or, if you want, I will get an arranger to write a lead sheet and send it to you but, if you will have time when you get back, that probably won't be necessary.

"Rigoletto," although it appears long, times out to approximately 3 minutes and 10 seconds. Regarding the "Barber of Seville," it also fits the music as I visualized it.

On "Puppy Dog," it requires just a simple melody patterned after "Two Front Teeth." I could perform it as a little kid, or it could be something for George Rock to do.

Also enclosed are the Billy Ekstine treatment of "Stardust" and the zany "Collector's Item." These are all I have *right now*, but if you would let me know of any ideas you have that you want me to work on, I will be happy to do so.

Incidentally, Joyce and I bought a house out in the valley in North Hollywood. It is 18 years old, but it is nice and solid and will be a comfortable place to store babies in (starting next year).

All my love to you and Helen and the gang. Hoping to hear from you soon.

Your friend,
Paul Frees

The Collector's Item

Everyone, they say, should have a hobby…
There's a million different hobbies to pursue…
From collecting keys to pens from hotel lobbies,
It all depends on what appeals to you… (Right?)

So who's to say that anyone is crazy,
As long as there's a pleasure that he gets…
If he has a passion for collecting sea shells…
Is he saner than a man who's fond of pets?

Philatelists have stamps from every corner of the world.
Hedda Hopper has a thousand different hats.
Who collects more funny jokes than that comic Milton Berle…
So what's wrong if I've an attic full of bats?…(Hmmm?)

Sydney Greenstreet has his recipes of things he'd like to cook.
James Mason has some thirty different cats.
Ethel Waters, as a hobby, has written a new book,
So am I crazy just because I love *my* bats?
If you'd only get to know them you would love them as I do…
Come on to my house now and I will show them all to you…

TALK: Here, here we are. (*Bats wings, squeals*) Here are my soft, sweet, furry friends. Hello, Boris (*Squeak*). Hello, Bela (*Squeak*). Hello, Borgia. (*Echo*) Don't be afraid. We scare them all! There, see, aren't they nice? Go on, pet them, see, they like you, they want to be blood brothers! (Laugh) I like you, too, so I'll give you a present, a nice soft furry coat of live bats. (*Laugh. Maybe they dance as Spike plays*)

Ed G. Robinson has paintings, collects all that he can get.
Mr. Belvedere has 60 pairs of spats.
J. Edgar Hoover keeps biographies of folks he never met.
So tell me, why do they think I'm insane…
That something is wrong with my brain…
Just because I am bats about bats?

(Builds...goes insane...)
Is it worse than loving your hats?
Pet lovers loving their cats?
Biologists loving their rats?
Gentlemen loving their spats? (*Laugh*)
Butchers collecting used fats?

(*Calm*) No!

TALK: Well, I gotta go now with my little winged friends. Wait for me, Boris and Bela, I'll fly home with you. (Big bat wings...echo and fade...) Goodbye...Don't forget to bite.

FINISH

Rigoletto (Defective Story)

Opening Fanfare:

HUMPHREY BOGART:	Say there, baby, have you seen this guy?
BETTE DAVIS:	What's he like?
BOGART:	He's a little over four feet high.
DAVIS:	Why do you ask?
BOGART:	You see, I am a very private eye and I have been hired by a client to try to locate this guy.
PETER LORRE: (Talk)	Why, that's me he is searching for! I will hide behind this potted palm and listen.
DAVIS (Picks up):	Well, why do you ask me? I am from society and I would hardly be caught in the company of such a hardened criminal character such as he.
LORRE:	Hardened criminal? Me? (Talk) I am just a lovable soul. I I wouldn't hurt anyone. I stab people in the back because I can't stand to watch their expression when they die.
DAVIS:	Why don't you ask that woman sitting there?
BOGART:	Would she know?
DAVIS:	Well, she knows everyone from everywhere.
BOGART:	Is that so?

DAVIS:	Why, she could tell you things to curl your hair, So I suggest you go and ask that woman there.
BOGART:	I thank you for your kind advice. I will see her right away.
DAVIS:	Oh, it was a pleasure, but please don't go, I think you're nice. I wish that you would stay.
BOGART:	I would like to know you better, but I must go.
DAVIS:	Oh, please…oh, no…
(Fast and build for duet)	
BOGART:	I think you are swell.
DAVIS:	I think you are grand.
BOGART:	It's been such fun.
TOGETHER:	But I (But he) must go. There is work that must be done.
(ALTERNATE:)	Goodbye (Goodbye) Farewell (Farewell)
TOGETHER:	Oh, it's been swell.
DAVIS DROOLS ON:	Why must you go. I want you. I need you. I love you. I will cry. I will sigh. I will die.
BOGART (Big):	*Aw, shuddup!*
VAMP TO:	
BOGART:	Excuse me, madame, don't think me rude But I am not trying to intrude. Could you say a few words? I wish you would.
LOUELLA PARSONS:	All right.

	Hello to all my friends in Hollywood.
	Now…what do you want of me?
	I mean ex*clus*ively.
	You will find that I will be
	Of any service that it is possible to be.
	(Talk) Just ask anyone in *Holly*wood.
LORRE:	She is telling him now where I will be found.
	He's turned his head and looks around.
	He sees me and I am in bad shape.
	I better make a break and see if I can *escape*.
BOGART (*Talk*):	There he goes! Grab him! (*Commotion*)
	(*Sings*) Now I got you, my friend.
LORRE:	I guess that this is the end.
	But tell me what did I do?
QUARTETTE SINGS:	Yes, tell us, tell us all, just what did this poor man do?
BOGART:	Do you recall a year or more?
LORRE:	Well, I'll try.
BOGART:	You were in Macy's (*Any big*) department store.
LORRE:	Yes, that is true.
BOGART:	You were shopping on the seventh floor,
	But they were out of the item you were looking for.
LORRE (Talk):	Oh, yes, I remember!
	(Sings) I needed underwear
	And I searched everywhere.
	They did not have my size.
BOGART (Talk):	That's right, buster.
	(Sings) So I have been sent out here by

	the store to apologize. You see, with Macy's it has always been a point of pride.
QUARTETTE:	Macy's sells for less.
BOGART:	Our customers must always be no less than satisfied.
LOUELLA:	They sold me this dress.
BOGART:	So forgive us, sir.
LORRE:	Oh, to be sure. You're not to blame.
BOGART:	Thanks just the same.
LORRE:	Altho I must admit you gave me quite a fright.
BOGART:	But the customer…
QUARTETTE:	The cherished customer…
BOGART:	The customer is always right.
ENSEMBLE:	(To big finish) The customer is always right. Is right. Is right. Is right. Is right.

Barber of Seville

OPENING:	Big operatic type fanfare…
GIRL (*Sings*):	Tell me, oh tell me, are you the psychiatrist?
DOC:	Yes, yes, I am, I am the man, yes, yes, I am!
GIRL:	Doctor…I'm not feeling very well…
DOC:	I can tell, I can tell, I can tell, I can tell. (*Fast*) Aha! What are your symptoms, where is the pain?
GIRL:	I got a pressure from men on the brain… In fact, I think that I am going insane.
DOC:	In other words, in medical terms, you mean you think That you are going nuts!
GIRL:	(*Talk*) Uh…yes!
DOC:	(*Talk*) Good! Now I take your case history… (*Sings*) Now, under what sign were you born, my friend…
GIRL:	It was under a sign marked *room for rent*!
DOC:	When you were born did you walk or fly…
GIRL:	I was so unhappy I'd always cry…

(MUSICAL BRIDGE TO VAMP)

DOC:	And what did you do, till the age of two?

GIRL: I sold peanuts at the local zoo.

DOC: (*Talk*) Aha! Maybe you have resentment to monkeys?

GIRL: (*Talk*) What do you mean I have a resemblance to monkeys?

DOC: (*Gets all flustered*) No, lady, you don't underst...I mean you got hostilities...that is you are, I mean is... (*He builds up real wild for*) Why do you hate your father?

GIRL: What?

DOC: Now I give you examination...
(*Sings*) Please be seated right where you are. (*Thump*)
Close your mouth and try to say ahh! (*Ah gagged*)
Look me straight in the fingers and try... (*Poke in eye*)
And jump off the chair and attempt to fly. (*Crash*)

Close your eyes, now what do you see? (*Scream*)
I take this hammer and hit your knee. (*Bang*)
How is your heart? Let's hear it beat... (*Tempo in time with this line*)

(*Slicker chorus here? Hmm?*)

GIRL: Doctor, I'm so dizzy I'm seeing spots...

DOC: I'm wearing a tie with polka dots...

GIRL: My head keeps ringing constantly...

(*Phone rings*)

DOC:	Well, answer it, I think it's for me… (*Talk*) Now we are almost finished. Now I straighten you out right away. I chiropract you vertebrae. (*Sound of bone?*) Now your ribs I tap and feel. (*Berry box crush*) Well, I see they ain't made of steel.
GIRL:	Doctor, are you almost through…?
DOC:	Yes, and I tell you what I'm going to do…
GIRL:	Is it anything to cause alarm?
DOC:	Nooo! All you need is a shot in the arm! (*Gun shot. Girl screams. Body falls*)

FINISH

"PARTNERS IN CRIME"
(JEREMIAH SHADE, ESQ.)

An Original Television Series Created and Written By

Paul Harcourt Frees

The desk clerk with the pencil-thin mustache stared at the incongruous twosome before him. "You want the *what*?" he asked quizzically. The short man in the bowler hat and high Hoover collar raised an eyebrow over bright grey eyes filled with assertive indignation and a slight amount of embarrassment. "The Bridal Suite! If you please."

"That's what I thought you said…," the clerk half muttered, and pushed the register toward them. As the mild-mannered little man sighed, he looked up lovingly at the long bone thin woman in the drab print dress standing next to him. Her faded blue eyes under thick octagon glasses stared at her diminutive escort with what was undoubtedly meant to pass for some form of passionate admiration, as she reverently sniffed at the gardenia corsage pinned to her lapel. The writing completed, the little man slid the register back across the desk, as she half whispered in a croaking voice… "Oh, Charles!" With this, the desk clerk looked up abruptly from the register and exclaimed suspiciously, "Charles, it says here your name is Mr. and Mrs. Phineas Finster." With that, the little man leaned forward onto the desk, and smiled benignly, "We eloped. You understand, don't you?" With that, the desk clerk, caught up in the spirit of the thing, smirked secretively. "Of course—hiding out from her old man, eh?" "So, if anyone comes here asking for us, you won't tell them, will you?" The desk clerk looked down and smiled shyly. "Course not, I get it," and with that, he summoned a bellhop and the middle-aged runaways were ushered to their Bridal Chamber.

Inside the room, the latter-day "lovebirds" waited until the bellhop checked the room, accepted the quarter tip, and had quietly closed the door behind him, before they broke from the tableau of "connubial bliss." Then, with a deftness and speed unbecoming of them both, they bolted the door securely, whipped open a small suitcase, set up a tripod for a high-powered telescope at the north window, and while the "Bride" waited, the small man in the bowler squinted through the eyepiece adjusting the instrument until, with a satisfied smack, he straightened up. The woman registered an almost immobile curiosity. "Well? Jeremiah?" she said. A satisfied smile crossed his thin lips, as he said, "I think we've located our elusive quarry, Jennifer, dear, now, let's see if we can bag him!"

And so begins another exciting excursion with the "PARTNERS IN CRIME." Jeremiah and Jennifer SHADE, the most unique detective team in the annals of Criminal Investigation.

Meet Jeremiah Shade, whose inconspicuous appearance and multilingual abilities have made him a Master in the art of surveillance, so important for the compiling of factual evidence needed to successfully conclude any criminal action. Not that he is incapable of handling himself should the need for physical dexterity be required—he can, although he prefers to work his way out of distasteful situations by employing more "civilized methods."

Yes, Law Enforcement agencies have required the services of Jeremiah Shade the world over, and where he goes, so does his talented sister Jennifer. Don't misunderstand; she isn't along for any ride. Jennifer's contribution has brought them safely through many a "distasteful" situation. Like Jeremiah, her unlikely appearance has proven to be an indispensable asset in their hazardous profession.

Unsuspected, they have moved in areas that the bravest police officer would never set foot into; undercover for the New York Police - a plot to blow up the Statue of Liberty on a busy Sunday afternoon; assignment to Italy's famed Carabinieri to protect a vacationing American Senator whose life is endangered; employed by the French Surete to help catch an International Smuggling ring to Hong Kong; as Innocent tourists to ALL the dark recesses of the World where crime festers and grows like poison mushrooms in a dark cellar.

This is the adventure-laden route that these two unlikely looking subjects journey upon! These are the dangers they face each time they accept an assignment.

These are the action-filled stories of television's most incredible team of Criminal Investigators. JEREMIAH SHADE and, his sister, JENNIFER SHADE.

"PARTNERS IN CRIME"

"WHO KNOWS"

Audition Script: July 9, 1956

A Pierce-Frees Production for Television (LIVE)

FADE IN ON SWIRLING MIST

RECORD - "HELLO OUT THERE" – Johnny Mercer

FADE TO BACKGROUND AFTER LYRICS OF FIRST CHORUS

SUPER TITLE OVER MIST

(Sponsor)   BRINGS YOU…

       "WHO KNOWS"

DROP SUPER AND FLIP TO

STARRING PAUL FREES

DROP SUPER AND FADE TO

AND HIS GUESTS: Professor Yale Mintz,
          DIRECTOR OF ASTRONOMY AT U.S.C.

START ROLL

Major Donald Keyhoe,
U.S. MARINE CORP., RETIRED –
AUTHOR OF *THE FLYING SAUCERS ARE REAL*

George Pal, PRODUCER OF SCIENCE FICTION MOTION PICTURES, *WAR OF THE WORLDS – DESTINATION MOON – CONQUEST OF SPACE* AND MANY OTHERS

AND

Jack Douglas, COMEDY WRITER.

RECORD HAS BEEN TIMED TO END VOCAL HERE

DROP ROLL AND DISSOLVE THROUGH TO PAUL FREES. HE IS SEATED AT DESK WITH MANY BOOKS, MAPS, AND PICTURES IN THE BACKGROUND.

FREES

There are many things, which we know to have happened, for which there seems to be no logical explanation. Things have disappeared—people have seen unidentified objects in the sky—houses have become known to be haunted by sounds and sights. Tonight, we will bring you three of these unexplained mysteries and we will ask our panel what they think actually happened, to give us—you and me—a believable explanation for these seemingly unexplainable phenomena. They have been vouched for by people who are experts in their fields—people who are above suspicion or exaggeration. We think the things you will see and hear tonight will surprise, please, and even shock you. We know the answers you will hear from our guest panel will amuse and amaze you, and now, I'd like you to meet them. First, from the University of Southern California, one of the leading astronomers and authorities on things astronomical today, Professor Yale Mintz.

CUT TO MINTZ – HE IS SEATED AT DESK

          MINTZ

Thanks Paul. I have accepted this invitation to grope with the unknown a little because I firmly believe that the biggest danger to progress there is, is the refusal to believe in the possibility of almost anything. I hope to be able to contribute something toward that theory tonight.

CUT TO FREES

          FREES

Thank you, Dr. Mintz, and next in line, a man who has been very much in the limelight the last few years for his controversial book, *The Flying Saucers are Real*, the man who was an advisor to Lindbergh on his famous flight to Paris, and a man who would be hard to dismiss as a dreamer—Donald Keyhoe.

CUT TO KEYHOE

          KEYHOE

That's very kind of you, Paul, and even though I know that many people have called me a dreamer, I am convinced that, whatever I may be, I'm right about the flying saucers. Time, of course, will tell.

CUT TO FREES

                    FREES

You've convinced me, Major, and when time
does tell, I know that *Life* will be there to get
the picture story. And now, our very special
guest from Hollywood—the person who
scared half the movie-going people in the
world out of their usual complacency with his
magnificent picture, *Destination Moon*, and
followed this up with *The War of the Worlds*,
Director, Writer, and Producer, George Pal.

CUT TO PAL

                    PAL

I don't think the people are really complacent,
Paul. I'm more inclined to believe that they
have been conditioned for years to believe
what they can actually see and understand,
and such things as life on other planets, or
space ships to the moon is simply not one of
those things. It's sort of like asking a man from
the eighteen hundreds to understand and
believe a guided missile of today. We know
they exist and we accept them. But, we've
been processed mentally by time, whereas the
man from a hundred years ago couldn't accept
this thing all at once. Frankly, some of the
things I've read in books about various phenomena, I find pretty hard to believe myself
even now, and I've been studying this kind of
thing for a lot of years.

CUT TO FREES

                    FREES

You'll have an opportunity tonight to disbelieve a few things, Mr. Pal, but I know you
will not find yourself at a loss for words nor a

good explanation. And now, last on our panel but certainly not least, our very good friend, the man who has probably thought up more explanations about more things than any of us because he's what is known as a comedy writer, Mr. Jack Douglas.

CUT TO DOUGLAS

> DOUGLAS
> Thank you very kindly, Paul, and I know it will come as a pleasant surprise to you, but I have read every one of your books.

CUT TO FREES

> FREES
> But I haven't written any books.

CUT TO DOUGLAS

> DOUGLAS
> That was the pleasant surprise I was talking about, but seriously, I've heard a lot of things said here tonight and I only wish one thing. I wish someone would tell me what I'm doing here.

CUT TO FREES

> FREES
> You're here for the same reason the rest of our panel is here, Jack, and right now I think we should get under way with our first situation. I'm going to tell an actual, documented happening and when I've finished, I'm going to ask each of you to explain what you think actually happened. There have been several so-

called explanations by so-called experts, but up to now these incidents are still among the unsolved mysteries of the ages.

ROLL FILM

RECORD MUSIC FOR NARRATIVE BACKGROUND

Our first incident: The mysterious disappearance of the British freight and passenger ship—the Waratah.

CUT TO FILM CLIP

PASSENGER LINER AT PIER READY TO SAIL – PEOPLE WAVING GOODBYE – SHIP PULLING AWAY

OFF CAMERA

FREES

July 26, 1909. Durban, Union of South Africa. The great new 16,800-ton steamer Waratah pulls slowly away from her berth, bound for Capetown. Commissioned a year before, she has already made two successful voyages from London to Australia around the Cape of Good Horn, and carries a Lloyd's of London classification of "100 A-one." With the exception of radio, she has every known signal and safety device available.

SHIP AT SEA PASSING ANOTHER FREIGHTER

On July 27, she speaks to the steamer, Clan MacIntyre. Her Captain reports all well, exchanges normal weather and destination data, and steams on her way down the well-traveled steamer lane.

SHIP LEAVING WAKE AND STEAMING

RECORD – AGENT

DISSOLVE THROUGH TO PRESS LOOKING DIRECTLY AT CAMERA

>And then she disappears. Just like that, the newest steamer with the newest safety devices known to man and 211 persons. She disappears without a sound or a trace.

CUT TO FILM CLIP - SHIPS AT SEA – SEARCH STUFF OF THE TIMES

RECORD – MUSIC TO MATCH

>The search is complete and continuous, but nothing is found. No debris, no wreckage, no bodies, nothing. Ships have gone down before, but always there has been wreckage, planks, steamer chairs, all evidence of a disaster. But as far as the Waratah is concerned, she might have been picked up by some great giant's hand and plucked into another world.

MUSIC – SWELL AND FADE

DISSOLVE THROUGH TO FREES

>Here are the facts, as we know them. The Waratha must have been within sight of land, yet she made no signals either by blinker or rocket. She launched no boats, or else they could have easily made land. The sea was heavy but not raging. No one, either on land or at sea, has ever come up with a trace of her, even the usual rumors about all disasters have never

turned up anyone who could bring any light on the disappearance. The court of Inquiry concluded that she had, and I quote, "Sufficient Stability as laden." Sufficient stability as laden or, in plain words, she was safely loaded. There was no reason for her to simply founder and sink without a trace. We can offer no more than the experts can but the facts are in and they challenge the curiosity of all. Perhaps one of the explanations offered by our panel tonight will help to solve this mystery, perhaps not. At any rate, it's open session now and I'd like to ask Professor Mintz for what he thinks might be the answer from his point of view.

CAMERA WORKS NOW COVERING FREES AND PANEL, AND CLOSE SHOTS OF MINTZ

MINTZ EXPLAINS BRIEFLY ANY THEORY WE MIGHT HAVE.

> FREES
> Thank you, Professor, and from the looks I see around the table here, you are about to be confronted with some, shall we say, varying theories. How about it, Mr. Pal?

PAL EXPLAINS HIS IDEAS, ETC.

EACH ONE IS ASKED TO GIVE HIS THEORY AND THEN WE CUT TO FREES

> FREES
> Fine, and certainly an interesting set of ideas. Now, since there seems to be come disagreement between these theories, I suggest we let our panel fight it out in the time remaining. Go ahead, gentlemen.

OPEN DEBATE ON THE SUBJECT

FREES INTERRUPTS

                    FREES
Time's up, gentlemen, and I'm sorry about it, too, because this has certainly been informative in more ways than one. To sum it up, we may not have contributed any facts that weren't around when we started, but there's been a lot of fruitful thoughts put on the table, and as long as people think, people will progress. If any of you viewers can add anything to our mystery of the Watarah, a letter addressed to:

SLIDE – "WHO KNOWS" – STATION _____
ETC.

        "Who Knows" – Station _____,
will reach us and certainly be acted upon.

                    FREES
Now—we have another mystery for the panel to discuss, and this one concerns a girl. A beautiful girl with long blond tresses who used to sit on a rock in the Mediterranean Sea off Greece somewhere and lure the sailors. Well, sir—it seems this kid suddenly disappeared one day, and our question is— where did she go? Any suggestions?

                  DOUGLAS
She got a better offer from Hollywood?

                    FREES
In a way, yes.

KEYHOE
They cut her hair and named her Marilyn?

FREES
No, not quite. As a matter of fact, what actually happened was that one day a great new tuna clipper sailed past the rock where the girl was working and instead of her luring the sailors off the ship, the sailors lured the girl aboard. And today, she's one of the best-known mermaids around.

DOUGLAS
I think maybe our boy has flipped his wig.

FREES
You don't believe me, Jack? I'll show you. I'd like to introduce Miss Chick of the Sea.

CUT TO MISS CHICK OF THE SEA ENTERING. SHE WEARS THE MERMAID OUTFIT AND WALKS ON STAGE. WE PAN, AS SHE CROSSES IN FRONT OF THE PANEL AND KEEPS RIGHT ON WALKING TO A ROCK WHERE SHE SITS DOWN.

FREES
This is a phenomena you'll see on this show that can be proved.

HE WALKS OVER TO HER AND SITS DOWN ON THE ROCK. THEY ARE COZY.

FREES
Tell me, Miss C, or can I call you Chicken— what's the good word from your end of town?

MISS C
Well, Paul, I guess you know about my family. Chicken of the sea and White Star Tuna. And, I'm

glad to report that they're all fine. In fact, better
than ever. You see, (INTO COMMERCIAL).

WE DO THIS COMMERCIAL BETWEEN PAUL AND MISS C.

AT CONCLUSION OF COMMERCIAL, PAULS SAYS HE'S GLAD SHE CAME BY AND TO GIVE HIS REGARDS TO ALL THE FAMILY AND SHE MAKES THE LONG CROSS AGAIN TO EXIT. THIS CAN BE QUITE EFFECTIVE IF SHE WALKS RIGHT. THE MERMAID I HAVE IN MIND DOES.

CUT TO FREES AND PANEL, THEN TO FREES

> FREES
> So now that we've had that little diversion, and I use the word little with a certain amount of reluctance, it's time for our second unexplained phenomena, and some more explanations from our guests.

ROLL FILM

MUSIC – TO MATCH

> FREES
> The case of Captain Charles J. Norcock and the mysterious "things" in the sky!

CUT TO FILM CLIP – JETS PEELING OFF IN FLIGHT

> This is a fantastic age we live in! Fifteen hundred miles per hour jets, guided missiles that destroy aircraft without human pilots...

SHOTS OF NINE HITTING BOMBER

> Great atom bombers that can circle the globe and carry atomic bombs to the ends of the earth.

SHOT OF B-36'S IN FLIGHT

    And most fantastic of all—flying saucers!

ANY SHOTS AVAILABLE OF SO-CALLED SAUCERS

    Since late 1949, persistent reports have been pouring in from every conceivable type of witness about strange things cruising about in our skies. Some are described as cigar-shaped; others like a great saucer. All reports have claimed incredible speeds and change of direction from the objects. The army has created and kept alive project saucers—to investigate these reports.

    Private individuals have challenged the army's findings – called them "cover ups" for news that might prove too shocking for the average American to take in stride. Some of us believe they are the result of hysterical imagination. Others think they exist, but that they are something the army is experimenting with—top-secret aircraft. One thing is certain: the flying saucers have made news and continue to make it. But this is 1954, when we can expect to witness things almost unbelievable. How about the sightings of strange things in the sky as much as ten years before the Wright Brothers made their first flight? Or the case of Captain Charles Norcock, in command of the British ship H.M.S. Caroline. At 10:00 p.m., on the night of February 24, 1893, steaming slowly through the East China Sea between Shanghai and Japan, Captain Norcock receives a report from the watch—"Unusual lights."

FILM OR MOCK UP SETS AND LIGHTS AS DECIDED

From the bridge of the Caroline, the lights are clearly visible. They are of a globular shape and seem to hover sometimes in a mass and other times strung out in a line just below the shadowy six-thousand-foot summit of land that marks the headland of the China Coast. For two hours, Captain Norcock and the entire personnel of the Caroline watch the lights string along in lazy flight, sometimes hanging almost motionlessly, then following a definite flight pattern in line across the pale blue night sky. Then, as though tired of this game, the objects strung out and bore northward until they disappear from sight over the horizon.

MUSIC – SWELL FOR BRIDGE AND FADE

The next night, the lights again are visible. This time, Captain Norcock trains his powered glasses on them and reports they are of a reddish hue and give out faint smoke. Moreover, the objects cast a reflection on the water below them. For a time, they disappear behind a small island but reappear, as the Caroline passes it. A few miles away aboard the H.M.S. Leander, a Captain Castle is observing the phenomena through his night glasses.

Curious, he alters the ship's course and makes toward them. The lights, as though fearful of closer observance, veer away and take an evasive course. In the log of the H.M.S. Caroline, there is a full report dated 1893. A written report was published in "Nature," May 25, 1893.

> There were, and still are, those who say, "Why couldn't these have been balloons?" Balloons carrying lights, traveling in procession and maneuvering over the lonely China Sea on that February night—ten years before the first man flew an airplane—a hundred feet at Kitty Hawk to make flying history. We don't know...

CUT TO FREES

FREES LOOKS AT CAMERA

> But we will ask our panel of guests—how do you explain this?

CUT TO DOUGLAS

> DOUGLAS
> Don't look at me. I didn't do it.

CUT TO PANEL AND FOLLOW AS BEFORE

THEY DISCUSS AND GIVE THEIR IDEAS ABOUT THE SIGHTING AND SUBSEQUENT SIGHTINGS. INCLUDE MARS THEORIES, ETC. AT CUE, THEY WIND IT UP AND WE MOVE IN TO FREES.

> FREES
> Fascinating. I think you'll agree with us on the saucers and that they will continue to make news, and, as they do, we will try to keep you posted.

ROLL FILM

> FREES
> Now, while our guests take a brief moment to gather their wits, let's take a look at something beautiful as well as necessary.

CUT TO FILM – TUNA CLIPPERS AT WORK, COMMERCIAL FILM

CUT TO PRESS

>   FREES
> That's the story and, for my money, it's a good one. Now, let's get onto our third phenomena and this one, we have an answer for, but our guests don't. We'll let them kick it around for a moment or so and then see who came the closest to the true explanation.

CUT TO SLIDE – CARTOON OF DOG CHAINED TO POST

> This incident concerns itself with a dog. A dog who up until the day in question had been a very well behaved dog.

SLIDE – CARTOON DOG. EARS UP, FEET OFF GROUND, BARKING LIKE CRAZY

> Then suddenly, our canine hero seemed to take leave of its senses. He started barking hysterically, strained at his tether and behaved like a dog with the screamie meemies. The lady of the house, not being able to calm her pet, rushed to the phone to call the veterinarian for help.

SLIDE – LADY PICKING UP PHONE. SHE'S PRETTY BEREFT

> But when she picked up the phone, low and behold, the dog stopped barking, and a voice on the other end of the line said, "Hello, hello, Mary, are you there?" When Mary, for that was the lady's name, said yes, she was there, the voice said it belonged to a friend of hers and that she had been calling Mary but no one had answered

for a long time. Well sir, Mary told her friend about her dog, her friend hung up, and that should have been the end of the little drama. However, it wasn't. The same day, the up-until-now happy dog suddenly took to the air again, at the same time letting out great barks and howls that lifted Mary right out of her chair. She tried without success to calm the dog and, finally, once again she made for the phone to call the vet, and what do you think happened? Right. As she picked up the phone, the dog stopped barking and sure enough, there was that voice on the other end of the line saying she had been trying to call Mary to find out how the dog was. Well, sir, Mary was pretty disturbed and to make a long story short, after this happened several times in the same day, Mary was ready for the booby hatch to say nothing of the good dog psychiatrist. Every time the same thing repeated itself. The dog started barking furiously. Mary picked up the phone, the dog stopped barking, and there was someone on the other end of the line. The phone bell never ran. Now then, what's the answer?

CUT TO PANEL AND FOLLOW AS THEY SPEAK

THEY EACH OFFER SOME EXPLANATION. IF WE HAVE A SPIRITUALIST, HE MIGHT SUGGEST THE OLD THEORY ABOUT DOGS AND EXTRA SENSORY PERCEPTION. AFTER THEY HAVE GIVEN THEIR THEORIES

CUT TO FREES

FREES

Well, I'm not just certain how the real answer will affect all of you good theorists, but for what it's worth, here it is. Incidentally, a case of (**sponsor's products**) is on its way to Mrs. Mary Goodwin for sending the story and accompanying newspaper clippings for us to use tonight.

Anyway, here is the payoff. When Mary finally called the vet, he suggested that she call the phone company. She did and they sent out a very nice young serviceman who checked Mary's phone and, what do you know, the electric current that normally rang the phone bell when somebody dialed Mary's number had become grounded in some way and instead of ringing the bell, it was shorting out to the post to which Mary's dog was chained. Yep – that's the answer. Every time the phone was supposed to ring, the electric current was going through the chain and into Fido and he, poor dog, was getting a jimdandy hot foot. When the phone was lifted, it cut off the current and all was well. Simple? Yes, like so many things once you know the answer.

If you viewers out there have any stories similar to this one, about anything that seems supernatural but has a logical but unexpected answer, send them to us and if we use yours, we'll send you a case of the finest (**sponsor's products**).

Now, since we have only a few minutes left, we'll take our cameras out into the audience for some questions for the panel. Let's go.

CAMERAS CUT BETWEEN AUDIENCE AND PANEL FOR QUESTION SEQUENCE

WE HAVE SCREENED THE AUDIENCE BEFORE THE SHOW AND ASKED THEM TO WRITE THEIR QUESTIONS ON A CARD. WE CHECK THE CARDS AND SELECT THOSE WE

FEEL ARE FITTING FOR THE SHOW AND CALL OUT THE WRITER'S NAME. WHEN THEY RAISE THEIR HAND, WE GET A CLOSEUP ON THEM AND LET THEM ASK THE QUESTION. THEN, WE LET THE PANEL GIVE A QUICK ANSWER. THE QUESTIONS SHOULD BE ALONG THE LINES OF "HOW DO YOU EXPLAIN THIS?" AND SHOULD DEAL WITH FACTUAL OR AT LEAST VOUCHED FOR HAPPENINGS THAT HAVE HAD NO ANSWERS.

THIS CONTINUES UNTIL TIME CUE, AT WHICH TIME FREES INTERRUPTS

CUT TO FREES

>   FREES
> Sorry, gentlemen, but our time is up. We have to climb on our tunas and hit for the open sea, but it's with a great deal of thanks that we say goodnight to our panel—Professor Yale Hints.

CAMERAS GET LINED UP AND ALTERNATE CLOSEUPS, AS EACH NAME IS CALLED

>   FREES
> Major Donald Keyhoe.
>
> Mr. George Pal.
>
> And Jack Douglas.

(EACH MIGHT HAVE A LITTLE GOODNIGHT OR SOME WORD FOR THOUGHT)

>   FREES
> And of course, we'll be back next week with some of the same members of the panel plus a couple of new names that I know you will all

enjoy hearing from. Until then, this is Paul Frees speaking, and wishing you all a pleasant goodnight.

CUT TO CLOSEUP CREDITS:

MUSIC – "HELLO OUT THERE"

(SPONSOR)

ROLL – A PIERCE-FREES TELEVISION IDEA

More Writings from the Bullwinkle Cast

Perverse, Adverse and Rottenverse
by June Foray

*Humorous essays from the voice of
Rocky the Flying Squirrel & Tweety's Grandma!*

Scenes for Actors and Voices
by Daws Butler

*Exercises & audition material from the voice of
Yogi Bear & Huckleberry Hound!*

Order now from
http://www.bearmanormedia.com

BearManor Media
P O Box 750
Boalsburg, PA 16827

BearManorMedia
P O Box 750 * Boalsburg, PA 16827

Welcome, Foolish Mortals...
THE LIFE AND VOICES OF PAUL FREES By Ben Ohmart

The official, heavily illustrated biography of the Master of Voice. Read all about the man behind the voices of Disneyland's *Haunted Mansion*, the pirates in the *Pirates of the Caribbean* ride, Boris Badenov from *Rocky & Bullwinkle*, The Pillsbury Doughboy and thousands of radio shows including *Suspense, Escape, The Whistler* and more.

ISBN: 1-59393-004-6 $29.95

Every old-time radio and cartoon fan in the world will want this book.

Foreword by June Foray. Afterword by Jay Ward biographer, Keith Scott.

"For the first time in print, the real Paul Frees is revealed. Author Ben Ohmart looks beyond the voices to uncover the man within, coming up with an evenhanded, but honest portrait of a very complicated individual. This is the definitive biography of an amazing artist."   – Laura Wagner, *Classic Images*

BOB AND RAY AND TOM by Dan Gillespie

This booklet is the first publication focusing specifically on Bob & Ray's writer, Tom Koch. Includes complete biography, information on the un-famous collaboration, list of published Bob & Ray works, and reproductions of Mad magazine panels written by Koch featuring Bob & Ray!   ISBN: 1-59393-009-7 $8.95

The Bickersons Scripts Volume 2 by Philip Rapp

Be the first to grab the NEW collection of Bickersons scripts! Includes squabbles from *The Charlie McCarthy Show* and *Drene Time*—plus never-before-seen commercial scripts (for Coffee Rich and other products) and the infamous Christmas episode written for the animated series! Foreword by Marsha Hunt.

ISBN: 1-59393-007-0 $18.95

Add $2.00 postage per book
For all these books and more, visit www.bearmanormedia.com

www.ingramcontent.com/pod-product-compliance
Lightning Source LLC
Chambersburg PA
CBHW022102160426
43198CB00008B/325